MYTHS AND MYSTERIES OF THE OLD WEST

MYTHS AND MYSTERIES OF THE OLD WEST

SECOND EDITION

MICHAEL RUTTER

TWODOT

GUILFORD, CONNECTICUT
HELENA, MONTANA

A · TWODOT® · BOOK

An imprint of Globe Pequot
An imprint and registered trademark of Rowman & Littlefield

Distributed by NATIONAL BOOK NETWORK

British Library Cataloguing in Publication Information Available

Library of Congress Cataloging-in-Publication Data

ISBN 978-1-4930-2828-3 (hardcover/paperback)
ISBN 978-1-4930-2829-0 (e-book)

♾™ The paper used in this publication meets the minimum requirements of American National Standard for Information Sciences—Permanence of Paper for Printed Library Materials, ANSI/NISO Z39.48-1992.

Printed in the United States of America

Thanks to Gary Frazier

CONTENTS

CONTENTS

INTRODUCTION

The Frontier West seemed endless, a land of adventure and opportunity. While dangerous and unforgiving, it was a rich country for a land-starved people. Hardworking men and women could make their mark in a world that typically didn't favor the commoner. Because the land was so large and foreboding, the men and women who rose to meet its Herculean challenges often loomed larger than life. Instrumental in forging and taming the West, such folk were not only an important part of our young country's emerging identity, they were a source of national pride. This nation valued and celebrated its heroic ancestry. We were proud that hard work, not birthright, determined a person's success. We were also a storytelling people, taking pleasure in tales about ordinary men and women who took on large challenges. The folklore of the West is as much a part of our heritage as the rugged landscape itself. Indeed the mythology that grew up around the facts often shaped public perception more than the truth.

The California Gold Rush, for example, helped define an emerging nation. Its beginnings were humble—men digging a trench for a sawmill. The strike held promise, but that wasn't enough. The gold fields of the Far West were "sold" to the American populace in one of the best public relations campaigns of the century. The result was a cross-continental rush for an elusive *El Dorado*. Fortunes were made on the western slopes of the Sierras, but the real treasure was the richness of the land. However, this wasn't the first time gold fever had struck. The legend of the Lost Seven Cities of Gold fueled the imagination of the Spanish conquerors several centuries earlier. The tall tales of a lazy priest, who told his superior that he'd seen the cities so he wouldn't be chastised, launched Coronado on his famous quest for fabulous fortune.

Continuing the quest for fortune in the West were the mountain men who probed its streams and rivers in the hunt for fur. Without doubt one of the greatest mountain men in our bounteous cultural legacy was John Colter. Here was a simple Kentucky lad, a backwoodsman, recruited by Lewis and Clark for one of the most famous expeditions in history. He couldn't get enough of the wonderful new land he helped explore, so he returned as a trapper. His escape from the Blackfeet is legendary. His bravery had been toasted and his exploits retold around many campfires long before any of the stories were written. He has also been credited, mistakenly, for discovering the Yellowstone National Park region that was later given the nickname "Colter's Hell."

Fox's *Police Gazette*, Beadle's dime novels, and casually written newspaper accounts, fueled by the public's desire to know about the West, made romantic folk heroes or villains out of Jesse James, Billy the Kid, Butch Cassidy, the Sundance Kid, Wild Bill Hickok, George Custer, Calamity Jane, and Buffalo Bill Cody, among others. Some like Wild Bill Hickok and George Custer had a genius for self-promotion, as well as a gift for telling an excellent story—

never mind that they played fast and loose with the facts. They understood the power of the press and used it to their advantage. They were held up to the public as paragons of virtue. Surprisingly Hickok, who was often portrayed as the man in the white hat, had more blood on his hands than Billy the Kid. He was deadly with his Colts, even if he wasn't a quick draw as one reads in dime novels. Nor did Wild Bill kill a hundred men as he had reportedly bragged—the number might be closer to seven or eight. And while Custer is known as a bold Indian fighter, he put his military career on the line and argued for better treatment for Native Americans on reservations. At one time Custer's reputation was nearing sainthood. Now his status is at an all-time low. He wasn't a saint, but he wasn't the bad guy we often think he was either.

Calamity Jane's reputation was also made by pulp fiction and dime novels. She was undoubtedly a brave woman and good with livestock, but she had a weakness for strong drink and that was her undoing. She was a tart, a braggart, and a blowhard. She might have had a successful career in Wild West shows, but she couldn't keep her bottle—or her mouth—corked. Nearly everyone she worked for, including Buffalo Bill, had to fire her for drunkenness. She tried to make it in a man's world, and, at least in legend, she succeeded.

Butch Cassidy, the Sundance Kid, and Etta Place naturally shied away from any sort of notoriety. Their reputations as Robin Hood outlaws developed first from the oral tradition, not self-promotion. As benevolent bandits, they cultivated the good will of the common people and were among the most successful thieves in the American West. Incidentally, there is no record of Butch or Sundance shooting anyone. Some very serious scholars argue that Butch and Sundance were shot to death or that their death was a murder-suicide in the face of overwhelming odds. These suppositions are very convincing; however, the romantic in us still hopes the two outlaw heroes lived to a ripe old age in the United States. And what happened to their charming consort, Etta Place? No one is really sure, but some say she was still living with Sundance in Mexico City a dozen years after his reported death in Bolivia.

Others like Billy the Kid, who didn't have much public relations savvy, were victimized as cold-blooded killers and outlaws by the press. Billy's biggest mistake was picking the wrong side in the Lincoln County War. He became the scapegoat for all the bloody violence in the region, but in truth he was merely a pawn in a larger power struggle. He wasn't the deadly left-handed killer of twenty-one men as we learn in traditional folklore. Besides being right-handed, he was a likeable young man who enjoyed singing, dancing, and gambling. He killed a couple of men, but he felt it was self-defense. Kid Curry, on the other hand, was a cold-blooded killer who was a true quick-draw in the Hollywood sense, both fast and accurate with his deadly Colt. Many historians argue that he was the most deadly, if not one of the fastest, guns in the West. At one time he was the most wanted man in the United States. He was a member of the Wild Bunch, and Butch Cassidy was the only man who could control him. Still, he had a gentle side not often seen— and a passion for fancy French underwear.

Sitting Bull became the whipping boy for the country's accumulated frustrations after the Little Bighorn. Some thought it impossible that an "uneducated savage" could defeat one of West Point's finest. Others wrote that he must have attended the Point incognito where he'd learned military tactics, which explained how he outwitted the US Army. Or, could this "heathen prodigy" have been trained in Europe before returning to his humble tribe? While such legends are amusing, the real truth about Sitting Bull, a great patriot chief, is of more interest. In his youth, he had more than sixty coups (war honors, often gained by striking a personal blow against an enemy). By the time of the great battle, he was considered a holy man and was known for his visions of the future. He had foretold the coming of the troops. His participation in the battle was mostly spiritual; he let younger chiefs, like Crazy Horse, lead the braves. While the Seventh Cavalry was wiped out, a number of the troopers' horses survived, including Comanche, perhaps the most famous cavalry mount in American history. This brave horse was badly wounded in the battle, but he recovered and became the regimental mascot.

The battle for the Southern Plains was a life and death struggle. Buffalo hunters were wiping out the herds at an alarming rate. To save their homelands, the tribes united and went on the warpath. The Battle of Adobe Walls stands out for several reasons. Between seven hundred and a thousand braves were fought off by a handful of hide hunters. And Adobe Walls was also where young Billy Dixon made the most famous shot in the American West. With his big buffalo gun, he reportedly shot and killed a Comanche brave nearly a mile away.

The worst wagon-train massacre occurred in southern Utah just before the Civil War. Approximately 120 men, women, and children were murdered. We've had well over a hundred years to study the tragedy, yet the circumstances are still shrouded in mystery. Did Mormon settlers in southern Utah participate in this slaughter?

The purpose of this book is not to tear down our mythology, but to refocus it. It's not surprising that our legends have loomed larger than life. From the tall tales told by the mountain men to the bravado of the dime novels and pulp fiction to Hollywood westerns, we love a good story more than a slavish adherence to facts.

The sin, apparently, isn't stretching the truth, but telling a bad story.

THE SEVEN CITIES OF CÍBOLA: THE LOST CITIES OF GOLD—THE MYTH, THE HOAX, THE LEGEND

Were there really lost cities of gold hidden someplace in the American West? What caused the Spanish to risk life, limb, and fortune to search for the Seven Lost Cities of Gold? And, has anyone ever found them?

There are few sirens more elusive than a lost gold mine, unless it's a lost city of gold. And there are few Western legends more tantalizing than the Lost Cities of Cíbola. Such lore was not only the stuff that dreams were made of, it was the stuff that fueled the first treasure hunt into North America (and many thereafter). In the 1540s, the great explorer Coronado nearly went mad as he pushed deeper into what is currently the United States in his frenzy to find the elusive cities. He never found his prize, but he helped carve out and establish a vast territory for his native Spain, a territory much larger than his homeland. He probably went as far north as Nebraska as he crossed the virgin land in search of fabled riches.

The legend of the seven lost cities of gold was born some years before the Spanish conquest of the New World, when the Moors were laying waste to Spain. The tale went that before the Muslim armies captured the fair city of Mérida, seven opportunistic bishops plundered the gold and riches from their respective churches— along with anything else that wasn't nailed down—and sailed away with the loot to "some mysterious land" to establish a new, wealthy Jerusalem. Supposedly, the seven bishops built seven neighboring cities, cities that became fabulously, indescribably wealthy. It was rumored that the streets were paved with gold, and that each house was embossed with tooled silver and studded with precious stones and gems.

After a century or so, the legend started to die down. However, when the conquistadors started to bring ship after ship of stolen gold from the New World, the legends concerning the cities of gold were rekindled. Many believed that the seven bishops really did establish their golden cities of Zion in the New World when they sailed off to escape the Moors. A man only had to find them and he'd be as wealthy as the pope.

Speculation ran high not only in Spain but in the Spanish colonies, as well. Many who had come to Mexico and South America believed that the cities would probably be found to the north, in the section of real estate we now call the United States.

In 1536, as the legend blazed hotter than the summer sun, four men stumbled into Mexico City, the new Spanish colony built upon Aztec ruins. The men, three Spaniards and an African slave, spun a tale about their wanderings for eight long years in the wilderness. They claimed that the Lost Cities of Cíbola—where buildings four or five stories high were made of pure gold—lay somewhere to the north. The four had never actually seen these structures, but they'd heard about them from natives. This was already a culture infected by gold fever, and it didn't take much to fan the blaze of rumor until it was a bonfire. This was, indeed, something worth looking into.

Nearly nine years earlier, in 1528, Charles V of Spain had sent five well-armed ships and a well-trained army (somewhere between three hundred and six hundred men) to colonize and conquer Florida and convert the Indians to Christianity. More importantly, he'd hoped to find gold. The Florida natives had other plans. They didn't view these men as great white gods. Nor were they interested in being converted to the cross, being murdered, or becoming Spanish slaves. In less than a year, disease, shipwreck, poor leadership, and native hostiles (the Indians reportedly fought like panthers) had taken their toll on the mighty Spanish. Charles's bold army of conquistadors was all but destroyed.

A few soldiers managed to escape the fierce warriors, the swamps, and the snakes, making it to the west side of Florida. In desperation they made several crude rafts and sailed into the unpredictable waters of the Gulf of Mexico. They knew that somewhere, thousands of miles away, was a Spanish settlement. Near present-day Galveston, Texas, they landed their roughly made rafts for the last time, planning to travel overland to the colonies in Mexico.

The local Indians were wary of the newcomers and quickly took them prisoner. Four managed to escape: a large African slave named Esteban (sometimes it's spelled Estavanico), and three Spaniards named Cabeza de Vaca, Dorantes de Carranza, and Castillo de Maldonado. For eight hard years they wandered through the Southwest and northern Mexico. They also visited the Gulf of California. Using sign language, they tried to communicate with the different tribes of Indians they encountered, always asking for news of a Spanish settlement. The slave Esteban took to living in the wilderness and found he got along well with the local tribes, who thought of him as a sort of medicine man. It's reasonable to assume that without Esteban the Spaniards wouldn't have made it. Somewhere in Arizona, possibly near present-day Bisbee, they heard of several large cities. Finally they reached a Spanish settlement in Lower California. After some rest there, they traveled on to Mexico City.

When they arrived there, the Viceroy of New Spain, Don Antonio de Mendoza, was keenly interested in their adventure. Publicly Viceroy Mendoza scoffed at the notion of lost cities. He suggested such rumors were, at best, pipe dreams and the colony shouldn't waste its time on nonsense. Privately, however, he tried to talk Cabeza de Vaca, who appeared to be the leader of the party, into leading an expedition back to the north to find the lost cities. Understandably de Vaca and the other Spaniards had had enough of the New World and wanted to sail for Spain as soon as a ship could be arranged. After eight years in a savage wilderness, from which they'd barely escaped with their lives, the three men wanted to enjoy civilization—chasing after treasure held no fascination.

Viceroy Mendoza bought the black slave, Esteban, from Dorantes de Carranza for a good price and secretly began outfitting a party to travel north and search for the cities with Esteban as guide. It had only been fifteen years since the greedy Cortez had laid waste to Mexico City, capturing vast amounts of gold for the honor of Spain. Mendoza knew that if he could replicate that achievement, he would be wealthy beyond his wildest dreams. He could not afford to have other men searching for the Lost Cities of Cíbola and risk having to share any of the wealth. So, rather than send a large party of soldiers on the trek, he would make his emissaries look like they were on a religious pilgrimage.

In the fall of 1538 or 1539 (the records conflict), he was ready. He chose a trusted Franciscan monk from Italy named Marcos de Niza to head the trip and told his associates that the expedition was for missionary purposes. "The cross," he proclaimed, "must be taken to the heathens in the north."

Monk Niza was fully aware of Mendoza's ulterior motive; nevertheless, he was willing to take Jesus to the tribes and be a missionary. It was his job to make a map of the area, so future parties could find the cities. It's likely that Niza was forced into this journey. The monk wasn't much of an outdoorsman, let alone a die-hard explorer. He put his faith in the guide, Esteban, who was, indeed, a man of the wilderness.

Esteban must have thrived on this adventure. His position as guide would have freed him, in part, from the literal and metaphoric chains of slavery that bound him. He would have gained respect and been almost on equal footing with the conquering Europeans. He also knew, as did Niza, that the expedition would fail without him. There wasn't a line of guides waiting to take his place.

Most Indian tribes had never seen a black person before, let alone one as large and strong as Esteban, and many thought he might be some sort of god. No doubt Esteban relished this new-found respect since it was antithetical to the way Europeans viewed members of his race.

Esteban instinctively understood the Native Americans. Unlike his Spanish companions, who considered the behavior of the natives beneath them, Esteban studied the tribes with the care of a cultural anthropologist. He understood their superstitions and customs. He worked at becoming a sort of itinerant medicine man (later on he claimed he was immortal). He dressed the part with bells and rattles and feathers. He carried several medicine bags with various items to impress his audience. It didn't hurt that he was at least a foot taller than the average brave and considerably stronger. The Indians showered him with gifts, including their young women. It was reported that he had quite an entourage—with, reportedly, many young women at his beck and call at one time.

Because of his rugged constitution and his knowledge of the wilderness, he was able to move much faster than the rest of the "missionary" party. Niza was in such poor shape that he couldn't keep up with his guide. He told the big slave to roam off ahead, talk to the tribes, and report periodically, either in person or by Indian runner. Since Esteban couldn't write, they came up with a plan should he happen upon one of the cities of gold. Too paranoid to trust such news to Indian servants, they devised a code. The messenger was to carry a cross if Esteban found one of the cities. If the cross was white, the locals were friendly. If the cross was black, the natives must be considered hostile. If the cross was a "span," roughly nine inches, the discovery was modest. If the cross was two spans, it was a good discovery. If the cross was three spans or more, the discovery was significant. Niza kept track of the guide's scouting progress while he relaxed and followed at a slower pace. He would hurry if and when the lost cities were found.

Near the New Mexico border in Southern Arizona, Esteban began to hear stories about the elusive cities. He kept searching north until he found the Gila River, where he stayed with some friendly Pima Indians. He enjoyed their roast dog, a special favorite of his, melons, and vegetables. This was the closest to heaven he had ever been: good food, respect from his associates, no white men bossing him around, and beautiful women. He lingered for a while, enjoying his stay among the cordial natives.

The Pimas told him of large cities, Zuni pueblos actually, beyond the headwaters of the Gila. Once he had enjoyed all the tribe had to offer, he settled down to the business at hand. After some investigating, he became convinced the Zuni settlements were the cities he sought. The Pimas offered to guide him. He was so sure the trip would be a success that he sent a tall white cross to Niza in his excitement.

With his Pima friends and guides, he traveled across the rugged Mogollon Range and then across the dangerous Apache territory. After a month of hard travel, more than three hundred rough miles, he reached the Zuni of Hawikuh (in present day New Mexico). It wasn't the city of gold as he expected.

Unfortunately poor Esteban was not so welcome here. The Zuni were not impressed by his "medicine," his manner, or his charms. Exactly what happened and the time frame in which the events unfolded is speculation. Unbeknownst to Esteban, the Zuni, unlike most of the tribes he had dealt with, were an unusually moral folk. They valued their women's chastity; virtue was an honored trait. Their religion was also more organized and didactic than most of the tribes. Apparently, they were not impressed by his eclectic trappings or his generic approach to the Great Spirit. Maybe Esteban was too forthright about his lustful eagerness, offending the Zuni and their principles of morality. Perhaps he assumed some of the garb and tokens from tribes he had met during his travels. It's speculation, but there's a good chance some of the amulets he'd sent to the Zuni chief, symbols of his mighty witchcraft and priesthood, were made by arch enemies of the tribe. As one would expect, this proved to be offensive, putting the already-skeptical Zuni leaders on their guard. We know he told the chiefs, either through sign or interpreters, that he was immortal and a mighty medicine man. The Zuni decided to challenge him and take him up on his boast. The dozens of stone-tipped arrows they shot into his body confirmed what they suspected—Esteban was as mortal as the next man.

The Zunis tried to kill the others in Esteban's small party, but a lucky few managed to escape. By this time the good monk was closing in, near enough to glimpse the fabled pueblos when he apparently encountered the few surviving members of Esteban's group running to safety. Niza realized that there was nothing he could do but turn around and run for his life, too.

"I pursued my journey," he wrote later, "until within sight of Cíbola." He continued, "The settlement is larger than the City of Mexico. I was tempted to go in."

Making himself seem braver than he was, the monk suggests that he wisely decided to come back. After all, if he should be killed no one would know about the city and how to get there.

Perhaps in the rising or setting sun, Niza thought he had indeed caught a glimpse of a golden sparkle in the city ahead. If you want something to look like gold, it will. And, hadn't his guide sent him a large cross? He knew that Mendoza would not be pleased if he found that the monk had sent his guide on ahead. To avoid trouble, Mendoza knew he had to bring back good news.

Likely, the priest doubted the authenticity of Esteban's report of finding the legendary cities at the moment of crisis. However, by the time he made it back to Mexico City, any doubt was gone. He had convinced himself that he really had seen a city of gold. When he talked to the viceroy, he told him the city he had seen was the least affluent of the seven (he apparently got this from the Indian guides who also managed to escape the Zuni wrath). Presumably a city named Totonteac was the largest and best of the seven, with "so many houses and citizens they never ended." He told his greedy, eager leader that he had made a cairn of rocks with a large cross on the top near the city, and had proudly claimed the cities "in the name of Don Antonio Mendoza, Viceroy of New Spain, for the Emperor, our lord, as a sign of possession."

The viceroy was greedy, but he wasn't stupid, nor did he trust the priest. Mendoza must have spotted a number of inconsistencies in Niza's story. For one, it must have seemed unreasonable that Niza would stop and build a cairn (to the glory of God) while being mobbed by angry Zuni. The good monk had obviously overplayed his hand, creating suspicions about the authenticity of his story. Viceroy Mendoza secretly sent a small group of well-armed men north to trace Niza's route. Mendoza wanted to be sure before he underwrote a costly campaign. For some time runners returned confirming much of what Niza had said. Then the reports ceased. In the meantime fresh rumors about a city of gold spread through the colonies. Mendoza was under a lot of pressure to do something. He waited as long as he could to hear from his men, but finally, fearing them dead, he gave up on their expedition.

On February 23, 1540, Don Mendoza commissioned Francisco Vásquez de Coronado to lead a large contingent of conquistadors. They rode to what they hoped was fame and fortune. To his dismay Niza was drafted as the party's guide. The priest was greatly disappointed to be heading off into this desolate land once again.

The procession must have been a glorious, if not an intimidating sight. At the front was a vanguard of four hundred soldiers in polished armor with plumes. Some rode trained chargers and carried heavy lances with banners. Others carried swords and crossbows. Behind them were seven to eight hundred servants and Indian slaves carrying gear. There were also carts of supplies, as well as herds of cattle, and even swine for the soldiers' meals. There were more than one thousand horses and probably an equal number of mules.

By summer Coronado found the first of Niza's Seven Cities of Gold. He ordered his men to attack without mercy, and the city fell quickly—men in armor with sharp Toledo steel were no match for Stone Age Indians. Where the mighty Coronado expected streets of gold and wealth beyond his wildest dreams, he found mud, adobe, and stone buildings several stories high. He wrote back to Mendoza, "Everything is the reverse of what he [Niza] said, except the name of the city and the large houses."

While Coronado knew that the monk had stretched the truth, he was still convinced that great rewards were to be had. The monk had lied about this village, but that didn't mean the lost cities of gold were not real. Coronado was jealous of Cortez, who had gathered wealth and brought an entire civilization to its knees. It was his goal to better him.

For more than two years, the disappointed leader and army continued to explore the vast new world in search of riches. Coronado and his tattered army returned to Mexico City. The expedition had been an expensive disappointment.

While the Seven Cities eluded the bold Coronado, to his dying day he was sure they existed. This driven conquistador was certainly not the last to hear the call. Like the music of the sirens, the addictive song of *El Dorado* whispered elusively from the next hill or arroyo, seducing the listener on. Coronado, though broken and broke, was one of the lucky ones. Most of the searchers ended up dead. While the results were often tragic for the treasure seekers, the results of their efforts were not completely in vain. A different kind of treasure was realized as a new land was discovered and laid open in North America.

THE BATTLE OF ADOBE WALLS: THE FAMOUS ONE-MILE SHOT

Did a thousand braves from the Southern Plains Tribes really attack a small outpost in the Texas Panhandle? Were a handful of men, about thirty, able to hold off the attack for several days? Did Billy Dixon, buffalo hunter, really shoot a brave a mile away with his trusty Sharps?

For decades the free-roaming Comanche, Southern Cheyenne, Kiowa, and Arapaho had been pushed into an increasingly smaller territory. Just as troubling were the dwindling numbers of buffalo, which were essential to the tribes' survival. When hide hunters started to invade the country around the Texas Panhandle (sometimes called the Staked Plains) to ply their trade, they threatened the last large herd of buffalo on the Southern Plains. Not willing to let the white man wantonly slaughter their food supply or invade their homeland, the Indians fought back with a vengeance.

A council of war was held in the spring of 1874 as the tribes camped near the Washita. Hide hunters had been getting bolder and bolder. Something had to be done. The buffalo was a way of life—providing food, clothing, and shelter. The free-roaming tribes were joined by reservation Indians who were fed up with confined living and federal promises. Many were starving because of bureaucratic corruption—promises were not enough to keep them alive. A so-called month's supply of rations was only sufficient for two weeks, thanks to skimming and payoffs. Worse, there was no way to supplement the food supply since the game near the reservations had been killed off.

In frustration tribes banded together, showing a great deal of cooperation. Traditional enmities were put aside as different peoples united against the common enemy, the white man. A young Comanche medicine man named Little Wolf emerged as a spiritual leader. He preached nationalism among the tribes, as well as a need for war against the invaders. Little Wolf had a number of visions that promised an Indian victory. He told the warriors he had a special medicine that would protect them from arrows and bullets. He promised the braves if they would paint their horses and war shirts they would be protected. Little Wolf called for an attack on the trading post at a place called Adobe Walls. In theory, at least, this was a wise suggestion since the supplies could be used to fuel further raids. The new trading post had more than one hundred thousand dollars' worth of provisions.

The Indians felt they were protecting their way of life, so they made preparations for war. They felt confident since only a few men guarded the post. Most important, a holy man had prophesied victory. (Little Wolf had even foretold that the warriors would kill the white men in their sleep.) The Indians were also well armed with the latest weapons, thanks to Mexican traders.

The hide hunters had been ruthlessly effective. By 1873 they'd nearly shot themselves out of a job. Since the Staked Plains region held the last big herd in the Southern Plains, the hunters eyed it greedily—the potential profits were big. Starting on the fringes of the region, they pushed deeper and deeper into Indian country.

The hunters and skinners would shoot and process hides until they had a load. Then they'd pack them into wagons and drive back to Dodge City to sell their take. After a night or two on the town, they'd buy supplies and head back for another hunting session. The trips back and forth to town took quite a bit of time. Some enterprising businessmen decided to open up a trading post in buffalo country and buy the hides for a fair price in the field, saving the hunters the trip. They could also sell supplies so the hunters could be provisioned. They'd carry everything a hunter needed—they'd even build a saloon. After some thought, the traders decided to open up an establishment at Adobe Walls, which was strategically located and a well-known landmark in the region. Almost four decades earlier, William and Charles Bent had established a trading post in the area. Later Kit Carson fought a battle on the site.

By the spring of 1874, the famous adobe walls were worn down but still standing. The traders set up shop nearby, a little closer to the creek. They constructed sod houses that were sturdy with good views. They built stores, a saloon, and a blacksmith's shop, among other buildings. The entrepreneurs brought in supplies worth a small fortune. Two partners, alone, brought in thirty wagons of provisions. Like the other principals in the venture, they planned to load up the empty wagons with hides and truck them back to Dodge. Then they'd fill the wagons with supplies and start the process over again. By May of 1874, the post was ready for business. And business was good—a number of hides had been taken in this buffalo-rich area. The hunters came and went, dropping off hides, picking up supplies, and some even came to the post to sleep. The Indians had begun to strike back and the hunters were on edge.

Nevertheless, danger was part of the buffalo hunter's stock in trade. The climate got more tense in June when several men were killed and scalped on Chicken Creek while their associate was at the saloon having a few drinks. Three more men were killed near Salt Creek. Others simply disappeared and were never heard from. Indians began following hunting parties. The Comanche and Cheyenne had a special dislike for buffalo hunters who only shot an animal for its hide, leaving the massive carcasses to rot in the sun.

By June 18 the traders had collected enough hides to consider taking a trip to Dodge City. Furthermore, there had been rumors of a possible attack at the end of June, making the trip to town more attractive than ever. Perhaps these warnings came from Kiowa dissidents who returned to the reservations after the war counsel. The partners didn't know if the information was reliable, but it would be foolish not to take precautions. The traders worried that if they made an attack public, the hunters might flee the post, leaving it especially vulnerable to attack. They also worried that they might lose face if they broadcast an attack—and there wasn't one. The principal partners kept the knowledge to themselves, not bothering to tell their associate, the blacksmith. Just to be safe, however, they conveniently decided that they would quickly head back to Dodge with the hides and leave Jim Hanrahan, trader and saloonkeeper, to watch the post and their affairs. A few days before the proposed attack, they took off for town.

At any given time, between twenty and forty men could be found about Adobe Walls. Whiskey consumption had gone up as the hunting slowed down. Some of the older hunters, many wise plainsmen, were being extra careful. The saloonkeeper playfully asked if they were running scared.

A young man named Billy Dixon and his two skinners had just come in with a fresh load of hides to sell. Jim Hanrahan bought the hides. Billy was known to be a good shot, as well as a hard-working young man. Jim took to him naturally. Billy decided to shift his hunting area, since the south was a bit too dangerous this season. Dixon's plan was to head off to the northwest, where the buffalo were thick and the Comanche thinner. Billy didn't have to work very hard to keep his skinners busy, so he and Jim entered into a partnership. Not only would Billy shoot for his own men, he'd also shoot for some of Hanrahan's skinners.

Neither knew it, but young Billy was about to become a very famous man. William Dixon was born in 1850. When he was eighteen years old, he started hauling supplies for the army. He worked for George Custer in the general's campaign against the Southern Cheyenne in 1868 and 1869. After a few years of freighting on the plains, he decided to try his hand at buffalo hunting. He joined up with some friends and became the shooter of the party. When the other regions were so shot out that he couldn't make a living, he came to the Panhandle.

Later in his life he would work as a scout for General Nelson Miles (Bear Coat Miles), Sioux and Apache Indian fighter. Billy would also survive the Battle of the Buffalo Wallow. In this battle he and five others were pinned down under Comanche fire. The group managed to make it to a buffalo wallow. Their water ran out and they were about to die of thirst when a freak storm blew in and a flash flood saved them. A wounded Billy crawled several miles and signaled a small army patrol that gave him supplies—which he took back to his men. As their last bit of ammunition was running out, they were saved by another patrol. Before he died in 1914, Billy wrote his life story. His wife published his book, *The Life of Billy Dixon*, after his death.

Jim Hanrahan was glad to have Billy for his partner. He was also glad that Billy and his skinners were at the post—extra rifles were comforting. Jim was probably kicking himself for not heading off to Kansas with the others, but his life savings were tied up in the saloon. He didn't want to abandon the valuable supplies he had accumulated. As the twenty-seventh drew near, he became more nervous.

According to legend, around two o'clock in the morning, a main roof beam snapped in the saloon. The men said the crack or snap was so loud it sounded like a pistol shot. They were awake instantly, guns in hand. Some of the men were sleeping in the saloon, while others had thrown their bedrolls outside since the night was warm. Fearing the sod roof would collapse, Jim, apparently, warned everyone to get out of the saloon. A few quick-thinking men grabbed a fork pole from a stack and quickly braced up the beam. Since the men were already up, most decided not to go back to bed. Dawn would arrive in a couple of hours and many, including Billy Dixon, would be leaving at first light. They talked, played cards, and had a few more drinks. Buffalo hunting was a lonely operation, so the hunters enjoyed the chance to socialize. When the pre-dawn attack came, the men were already up. There was no morning grogginess or indecision to slow them down. The men later felt the cracking beam had saved them from massacre.

Was the broken beam just a fluke? Some students of this battle wonder if Jim, justifiably nervous about the predicted morning attack, fired his pistol into the night to arouse the sleeping men and to get them ready. He dared not tell the hunters he had knowledge of an impending attack, but he had to get the men up somehow. A shot in the dark, if that is what happened, proved to be a good idea.

If nothing happened, he'd be out a bullet, a few hours' sleep, and some watered-down whiskey, but if an attack occurred, being up might save the men's lives. There is merit to his thinking. No one seemed to wonder why Jim was fully dressed with his boots on when he shouted that the beam was cracked. Everyone agreed the crack sounded a lot *like* a pistol shot, but no one thought about it after he shouted that the main beam was cracking. A problem with the main beam in a sod house wasn't uncommon in that day; thus, no one stopped to question the saloonkeeper. Had the men been of a more questioning nature, they might have noted that it was out of character for the bartender to pass out free drinks so generously. He never gave anything away. If Jim had staged the incident, he'd want to keep them up and socializing. It was said that if a man thought he might curl up in his blanket for an hour's sleep, good ol' Jim filled his tin cup with red eye.

That night the Indians camped a few miles to the east of the post, confident of the outcome. They sang war songs and prayed to the Great Mystery for the promised victory the next day. Their medicine was good; their war paint was magic. Written accounts tell of at least one thousand anxious warriors ready to kill and plunder the unsuspecting post. This number was certainly exaggerated in the retelling. No doubt it seemed like a thousand warriors to the twenty-eight defenders. In reality, there were probably between five hundred and seven hundred attackers, which was still quite a large number for those times. Well before dawn the braves were in place and ready—although unaware that the men at the post were awake. After all, Little Wolf had told them the hunters would be sleeping and the victory would be theirs.

If legend is correct, Billy Dixon was the first to see the attack. He was securing his horse, getting ready to leave, when he saw the charge. At first he thought the braves were going for the horses. He fired a couple of rounds at the lead warriors, which alerted the post. The braves, however, bypassed the horses and went for the buildings. Men scrambled for shelter. A couple of those still sleeping outside were killed. Billy made it to the saloon. Others took refuge in the stores. The buildings were well built, and the men further secured the doors and windows with barrels and sacks of supplies.

The braves didn't get the quick victory they had hoped for. These were tough plainsmen who didn't frighten easily; they were cool under attack. Furthermore, buffalo hunters were notoriously good shots. They were used to making each bullet count and firing from a distance. Even the skinners were excellent shots. During the first charge the braves were literally upon the buildings, so the defenders shot from the windows and through holes they opened in the walls of the sod houses. Because their fire was so deadly, they turned back the first rush—a rush that should have brought victory to the braves. More charges followed, but each one was repelled by the men's rifle fire.

The men in the saloon realized they were starting to run short of ammunition, so Dixon and Hanrahan dodged bullets as they ran for the store so they could replenish their supply. Billy decided to stay in the store while Jim ran back to his saloon. Before noon, the braves had learned a healthy respect for a buffalo rifle and had given up charging. The Indians were losing their zeal for this fight. They had taken horses and a few supplies that had not been unloaded from several wagons. They managed to kill a few of the white men, but this was not what they had been promised by their medicine man. Even the great chief of the Comanche, Quanah Parker, had been hit; luckily, though, the bullet was nearly spent and didn't break the skin. Still, he was injured enough to be out of the fight. The traders and buffalo hunters were bottled up, their horses gone, but they had the essentials: food, water, bullets, and whiskey. They were safe for the time being, although they couldn't go anywhere. During the battle, several other hunters had slipped into the post between raids to bolster up the defenders. During the night of June 28, several men snuck out for help.

Now it became a waiting game. Bored with just sitting there, Billy decided to take a shot at one of the Indians sitting on his war pony. The man was well out of range, but Billy decided to stir things up. As it would turn out, he was about to make the most famous shot in the history of the American West. Using his Sharps .50/90, he calculated wind and distance. The other men watched, not having much else to do, agreeing the brave was about a mile away. No one questioned that Billy was a fine shot. Any man who could kill buffalo the way he did was a shooter. Billy carefully took aim, held his breath, and squeezed the trigger on the trusty Sharps. The black powder smoke cleared and the men watched for several seconds. Almost in slow motion, the unlucky brave threw up his arms and fell from his warhorse. This was the best shot any of them had ever seen or hoped to see. Drinks flowed to celebrate the shooter. Later some curious surveyors measured off the shot. It wasn't quite a mile, but it was close—1,538 yards.

To Billy Dixon's credit, he never claimed it was more than a lucky potshot he took to break the boredom of the long siege. He called it a scratch shot, but Billy knew his craft. How many buffalo he had killed with his heavy Sharps can only be speculated—certainly in the hundreds, possibly in the thousands. He knew his weapon, made his living by it, and had fired until the barrel was hot many, many times. The buffalo hunters were so deadly that the Comanches mostly kept to three hundred yards away after the first morning. Even a three-hundred-yard shot at a moving target is something to brag about. That twenty-some men could keep off five hundred or more attackers says something about their marksmanship.

As soon as reinforcements arrived, the battle was officially over. The Indians broke into smaller bands and went on a bloody rampage in a four-state area—Texas, Kansas, New Mexico, and Colorado. They had lost this battle and would soon lose the war, but not before they made their anger known. Perhaps as many as one hundred whites were killed over the next two months. The prophet, medicine chief Little Wolf, was dishonored and ostracized by the Comanche people. He became known as Coyote Droppings. He always claimed that the braves had broken his magic when they killed a skunk on the way to the battle.

The traders and buffalo hunters won what has now been called the Second Battle of Adobe Walls (the first battle, previously mentioned, was fought in the same location years earlier). Even though they succeeded in driving off the Indians, the traders decided that

Quanah Parker, Comanche Indian chief

Adobe Walls wasn't a safe place to have a post any longer. By July 5, even saloon owner Jim Hanrahan abandoned his establishment, loaded up his supplies, and slipped back to Kansas with a heavily armed party of men. As soon as the post was abandoned, the Indians burned what remained. Most people have forgotten the saloon keeper's name but still celebrate Billy Dixon as the man who made a shot that was nearly a mile away.

Buffalo bones c. 1870

THE MYTH OF THE ONE-MILE SHOT

More than 130 years later, one wonders if Billy Dixon really did make such a shot. Was it possible? Or was this just another tale one could chalk up to old-timer whiskey talk? Did Billy Dixon, buffalo hunter, really kill a Comanche Indian 1,538 yards away with his .50/90 Sharps rifle?

Keep in mind that Dixon was shooting a 675 grain bullet. The average deer-hunting bullet nowadays, by comparison, averages around 150 grains, considerably lighter. Note, too, that the velocity of Billy Dixon's round would be approximately 1,216 feet per second. Compare that to the average 3,000 feet per second of the modern deer cartridge. He was shooting a slow, extremely heavy round. We know that military personnel after the last World War, presumably with a fair amount of practice, often shot at man-size targets at 1,000 yards with open sights using a 30.06 Springfield. Long-range, open-sight shooting, therefore, can be done.

Mike Venturino, the acknowledged expert on black powder cartridges, nowadays, set out to see if Dixon's shot was technically possible. Using a Sharps .50/90 with a 675-grain cartridge, he set out to bust or prove the frontier myth. He was accompanied by scientists in Arizona with radar equipment so they could do tests on the bullet. Some have speculated that a bullet this heavy could not actually travel the nearly 1,600 yards, let alone have enough force to kill. What the experiment proved was that, technically, such a shot was possible. If a shooter elevated the barrel of the Sharps thirty-five degrees, the bullet would go 3,700 yards. The studies proved that even if the barrel on the heavy old Sharps was held up five degrees, the bullet could still travel 1,517 yards. The weapon was indeed capable of such a shot.

JOHN COLTER: MOUNTAIN MAN AND EXPLORER

Did John Colter, the famous mountain man and Lewis and Clark alumnus, really discover the Yellowstone country? Was "Colter's Hell" in Yellowstone Park Colter's discovery? Was John Colter responsible for the wrath of the Blackfeet Indians?

In 1806 the Lewis and Clark Expedition was on its way home from the Pacific Ocean after a two-year journey across the newly acquired Louisiana Territory. Most of the men were ready for a soft bed, a bath, and a decent meal after the privations of the trail over the past months and years, so it was surprising when near the Mandan Villages in North Dakota, John Colter agreed to join a small group of men who were headed for the upper Missouri to trap for beaver. It would mean spending another long winter away from home. Because of his excellent service, he was given permission to leave the expedition early. As Lewis and Clark reported in their journals, "Any one of our party who had performed their duty as well as Colter had done" could go with the leaders' blessings.

John Colter was one of the most daring mountain men in the history of the American West. As an original member of the Corps of Discovery, traveling with Lewis and Clark on their history-making expedition across an uncharted continent, Colter was a valued member of the party and is noted in history books.

His contributions as a trapper and explorer after the Corps of Discovery went home, however, are not as clearly defined.

Popular legend has Colter discovering Yellowstone Park, specifically the Geyser Basin region, referred to as "Colter's Hell." Furthermore, this bold mountain man is also said to have helped incite the long-running war with the Blackfeet Indians. Here again fact and legend play loosely with one another.

John Colter was born in Virginia in 1775. He learned how to hunt and shoot at an early age and seemed to take to the woods quite naturally. In the autumn of 1803 in Maysville, Kentucky, when he was twenty-seven years old, he enlisted in the army—recruited by William Clark. This small army was going to be part of a special expedition headed by Meriwether Lewis. The men weren't sure what they were getting into, but the trip promised adventure and excitement.

John Colter could be a hard-drinking, rowdy man, and he was reprimanded more than once for not corking a whiskey jug. Nevertheless, once they were on the trail, he proved to be a valuable addition to the Corps of Discovery. He was resourceful, tough, and a fine woodsman. He could also be trusted.

Colter and his friend George Drouillard became the company hunters. They ranged widely in their search for meat to sustain the party. Colter, like Drouillard, was able to take care of himself in the wilderness and was gone for days at a time. He supplied tons of meat for the party and was asked to perform a number of dangerous, sensitive missions and assignments.

After agreeing to return up the Missouri with the small band in 1806, Colter discovered that he didn't get along with his new partners. He left them as soon as the spring thaw opened the rivers.

The spring of 1807 found him paddling his canoe down the Missouri River toward home, once again. Near the confluence with the Platte River, Colter saw a number of keelboats tied up on the bank and went over to see if he could scrounge up a meal. To his surprise he found several of his Corps of Discovery comrades, including his good friend and fellow hunter, George Drouillard. His friends were part of a group headed by the bold but disagreeable Manuel Lisa. They were bound for the far mountains to hunt beaver. Since Colter knew the land, Lisa persuaded him to come along as well. Colter was probably no fan of Lisa, but he loved the mountains and was eager to be with his friends and go on another adventure.

We know some of the places Colter visited during his backwoods odyssey. He had an eye for detail and a good memory, identifying a number of lakes, rivers, ranges, and geographic features that make tracing some segments of his sojourn relatively easy. Other parts of his adventures, however, are subject to debate. A number of theories abound about his sensational wilderness adventures—but they are only theories, because he was pretty much on his own from August 1806 until May 1810. His skill was nonpareil; the mountains would have claimed him otherwise. He lived to tell tales of a fantastic, dangerous land. In spite of Colter's fame, we don't know as much about him as we'd like. He left no written record about his Rocky Mountain years, and, sadly, he died rather young. We've pieced together a number of his oral tales. We have accounts from Lewis and Clark, Henry Breckenridge, and Manuel Lisa, among others. There are also the detailed accounts from Clark, who interviewed Colter in some detail in 1810 for *Maps of the West* (published in 1814). While Clark's accounts are helpful, they do lead to further speculation. There are a number of inaccuracies that have led to different interpretations. Thus two hundred years later we still have as many questions as we have answers. For example, did Colter get as far as South Pass? Did he cross the rugged Wind River Range in the winter—which would have been a Herculean achievement? We just don't know.

We do know he made his way up to the Jackson Hole region, where he admired the rugged peaks and hiked the shores of Jackson Lake. He may have made his way over Teton Pass into present-day Idaho, but we're not sure. Eventually he snowshoed up the north side of Yellowstone Lake and went up the Yellowstone River to the falls. We know that he then made his way toward present-day Cody, Wyoming, and spent some time on the Shoshone River, which was called Stinking Water on Clark's map, aptly named for the foul sulfur dioxide, rotten-egg smell and smoke that permeated the area. The area was geothermally active in Colter's time, although it's not particularly active today.

After Colter's death, Stinking Water, with its haunting vapors and stench, became known as the famous "Colter's Hell." While the true Colter's Hell was outside of Cody, it was also erroneously associated with an active geothermal area in the northwestern section of Yellowstone National Park. As far as we can tell, the writer Washington Irving was the first to coin the term "Colter's Hell" in his book on Captain Bonneville in the late 1830s. Irving wrote that the Stinking Water held "gloomy terrors, hidden fires, smoking pits, noxious streams, and the smells of brimstone." It wasn't until 1895 that Hiram M. Chittenden perpetuated the false mythology in his book *Yellowstone National Park*. He called the Geyser Basin Colter's Hell. This was an honest error on his part, but the name caught on. For more than a hundred years now, folks have equated Geyser Basin with John Colter. While he traveled a great deal, Colter never actually made it to that sulfurous section of Yellowstone National Park. Chittenden corrected the error, incidentally, in his next book, a book worth reading, called *American Fur Traders of the Far West*. Colter's place in Yellowstone folklore had already been sealed, however, and the legend continues to this day.

Colter continued to trap for Manuel Lisa from the fort that served as the company's headquarters. At Colter's suggestion the trappers befriended the Crow Indians, but the Crow were at odds with the Blackfeet. The Blackfeet had always been proud and independent, lording their might over smaller, less powerful tribes. Because of a trade agreement with the British, the Blackfeet were the first tribe in the region to have modern weapons, and they did their best to keep them out of the hands of other tribes. The Blackfeet literally outgunned the other Indians in the area.

The Blackfeet didn't mind trading—as long as it was done exclusively through them. They wanted a monopoly on commerce. They were angered when William Clark told Blackfeet leaders that soon Americans would be in the mountains to trade with the Shoshone and Flathead tribes, as well.

On their return, Drouillard and Lewis had a skirmish with the Blackfeet. They awoke in camp to find several braves trying to steal their rifles. Reuben Fields ran after a brave who had taken his rifle and buried his knife in the warrior's chest. Lewis gave chase to a man stealing his horse, brandishing his pistol. The warrior turned to fire so Lewis gut-shot him.

This was the beginning of an all-out thirty-five-year war between the Blackfeet and the Americans—a war that would be further inflamed in the next few years by John Colter. In 1808 Colter was crossing present-day Bozeman Pass when he joined a group of Flathead Indians heading off to the plains to hunt buffalo. This was a risky operation for the Flatheads since the plains and the buffalo were jealously guarded by the warring Blackfeet. Not surprisingly, they were attacked by a Blackfeet raiding party.

Folklore has Colter fighting like a maniac (which was probably true, considering the alternative) before finally taking a ball. In spite of his wound, he continued to fight. He could fire and reload quite rapidly, which amazed the braves on both sides. The Blackfeet got a good look at the white fighter and were eager to take him captive—white men were pretty rare in these mountains. During the battle Colter was seen killing a Blackfeet warrior. From that moment on, the surviving Blackfeet braves remembered him and wanted to even the score. Fortunately a large group of Crow warriors came to the rescue of Colter and the Flatheads, driving the Blackfeet away. Colter was taken to Fort Raymond where he recovered from his wound. Nevertheless, he was now a marked man.

The next year Colter and his friend John Potts were canoeing into the headwaters of the Missouri when they had a stroke of bad luck. As they paddled up the Jefferson River, they saw a large party of Blackfeet warriors on the east bank. Colter was closer to the bank than Potts, but they were both within rifle range. There was nothing to do but surrender. What happened next has been retold and embellished so often we don't know what is truth and what is fiction. We're certain that something happened on the banks of the

Jefferson, but we're not exactly sure *how* it occurred. As a mountain man, Colter wouldn't have hesitated taking a bit of poetic license as he retold this tale. No doubt there have been creative additions as others retold it. Telling a good story was more important than slavish adherence to something as trivial as fact.

Colter must have been tempted to go for his rifle, but he knew better than to try to fight such a large band of armed Blackfeet. Legend has it that there were more than two hundred warriors on shore. Potts was a little farther from shore and decided he had nothing to lose. He grabbed his flintlock, but before he could get the rifle up or cock it, he was killed by a barrage of Blackfoot lead. The warriors took Potts's body, scalped him, and then mutilated his corpse. Several of the braves had recognized Colter from the previous year, and they had something special in mind.

Colter was taken to the nearby camp and stripped naked. According to Blackfeet custom, since he was a brave man, he wouldn't be killed outright. He'd get a chance to prove his bravery. They gave the naked, unarmed Colter a five-hundred-yard head start, and then came running after him. John Colter took off.

Unlike many mountain men, Colter was a walker and in wonderful shape. Even without moccasins, he was able to out-distance all but a few of the braves. Before long his feet were mangled and shredded beyond recognition on the sharp rocks, thorns, prickly pears, and sticks. But so far he was staying out of range of the arrows that were fired at him.

After a few miles he had pulled away from all but a few of the best runners. One brave carrying a war lance was able to catch up with him, but when the man got close, Colter tripped him and wrestled the lance away. He picked up his speed to keep his distance. He got to the icy Madison River, plunged in, and managed to stay hidden, upsetting the Blackfeet who searched the banks carefully. Legend has it he was able to avoid detection under a stack of driftwood, just keeping his nose up for air. He may have hidden in a broken-down beaver lodge.

Once the Blackfeet had given up, the half-frozen Colter crept out of the water and put as much distance as he could between him and those who wanted his scalp. His feet were in awful shape. All he had eaten for days was roots. Seven long days later, still dodging Blackfoot war parties eager to nail up his hide, he made his way back to Fort Raymond—more dead than alive. The Blackfeet were angered that Colter had broken free. From that point on, there were no more cat-and-mouse games. Any white man captured by the Blackfeet was tortured and killed.

After Colter's last incident with the Blackfeet, he was more cautious. He knew he'd pushed his luck. The average time a mountain man lasted in the wilderness, thanks to grizzlies, Indians, disease, and accident, was a year. After the rugged Lewis and Clark Expedition, Colter had spent another four years in the mountains. He loved the lonely, wild life, but he must have felt he was pushing his luck.

In 1810 he headed down the Missouri River for civilization, and he stopped to visit his old friend Captain Clark. Clark was preparing a large map of the western regions, and Colter was especially helpful with information about the southern tributaries of the Yellowstone.

Captains Lewis and Clark holding a council with the Indians

That year he found a nice girl named Sally, settled down on the Missouri frontier, in Franklin County, and became a yeoman farmer. He had a son and enjoyed life at a slower pace. His neighbor was Daniel Boone, the aging frontiersman. The chats those two must have had! Colter was severely jaundiced at the time of his death, but the cause of his death in November of 1813 is unclear. He never lived to see forty, but he had filled his life with excitement and adventure. John Colter was one of the great pioneers and explorers of his age.

THE CALIFORNIA GOLD RUSH: THE GOLD DIGGER'S WALTZ . . . GOLD! GOLD! GOLD!

Was the California Gold Strike an instant draw? Was it the largest strike in the American West, and how was it brought to the attention of the public? Was gold found at Sutter's Mill by accident?

Those fateful words, "Gold! Gold! Gold! Discovered on the South Fork of the American River," set off one of the largest human avalanches since the Crusades swept across the Holy Land. By the fall of 1848, more than ten thousand men were chasing the dream of *El Dorado* in the foothills of the Sierra Nevada. By 1849 more than thirty thousand men sailed to California, while another forty-one thousand trekked overland. Within a dozen years there would be four hundred thousand miners looking for that elusive pot of gold.

Gold fever swept the nation, and everyone wanted a share—or at least to read about it. Newspapers, even so-called respectable papers, tried to outdo the competition, printing fantastic stories. Interestingly enough, some were actually true or based on truth. All fueled the lust for a quick fortune. One paper's lead article told about a hungry hunter who shot a bear near the Tuolumne River. The dying beast tumbled over a small cliff and landed on a ledge. When the hunter went to retrieve his game, he looked up at the wall and saw a wide vein of quartz sandwiching a rich find of pure gold. Another paper wrote about a claim making forty thousand dollars a day. A newspaper's "bread-and-butter" stories were first-hand accounts, often taken from letters. Here are several examples: MY LITTLE GIRL HAS MADE $25 A DAY PANNING FOR GOLD! MY INCOME IS $150 A DAY ON MY CLAIM! I TOOK $1,000 FROM ONE PAN FULL!

To the Yankee brought up in the land of opportunity, this boon from a smiling providence was the Holy Grail. However, simply getting to the gold fields was at least half the problem. Both sea and overland pilgrimages were fraught with peril. Those who couldn't wait for spring and had a nest egg burning a hole in their pockets hopped on whatever ship was available. They could sail around the Horn for San Francisco, which was an eighteen-thousand-mile trip. Or a traveler could get off in Panama—which cut the trip in half, but added the risk of tropical diseases—in addition to the risk of traveling by mule and canoeing across the isthmus, and then hoping to catch another ship to California.

Sea journeys were quite rough. In the hopes of making a large profit, many captains and ship owners filled every corner of their vessels. Supplies were literally worth their weight in gold, but greedy owners would not turn down cash-paying customers. Food and water on the voyage were bad. Sickness, because of the overcrowding, was a common occurrence. Going overland was not without serious risk either. In April of 1849 a horrible cholera epidemic hit many wagon trains.

Besides disease, there were the physical elements of wagon travel: broken wheels, flooded rivers, steep mountains, livestock issues, restocking supplies, and Indians.

While it did become a mass migration, the beginnings of the California Gold Rush were considerably more humble. The "Gold Fever" concept was really one of the more successful advertising campaigns in Western history—pushed by both business and government. Without this "extra" help, there still would have been a gold rush and it would have been large, but it wouldn't have been a national obsession.

As so often happens, the men who were responsible for the discovery of gold in California were not able to capitalize on their discovery. John Augustus Sutter had knocked about the Far West for nearly ten years before he decided to settle down and carve out his own empire in the California wilderness. He built his home on a rich section of land in the Sacramento Valley in the late 1830s, close to the Sacramento and American Rivers. Being a cautious man, he constructed a fort—Fort Sutter. Within a few years, his settlement thrived. He built a mill, a tannery, and a winery among his other concerns. He planted wheat in the fertile fields and developed herds on the rich pasture land. He hired local Indians for labor. The Swiss-born Sutter made a comfortable, prosperous life for himself. He raised enough for his own needs and sold the surplus to the other settlers who had begun to populate the area.

After ten successful years, Sutter had prospered to the point where he needed a lumber mill to provide materials for his expansion plans. Besides, it would be good business. He could make a small fortune selling his lumber to his neighbors. Since Fort Sutter was built on the plains, there was very little useable timber nearby, and although Sutter knew of several good places to cut lumber, he didn't have time to do the work himself. He enlisted the help of

James Wilson Marshall. He sent Marshall to scout out locations for the new mill. With Sutter's blessings, Marshall decided the best location was about forty miles to the northeast on the South Fork of the American River. According to their agreement, Sutter would underwrite the cost of the mill, and Marshall would run the day-to-day operation. By the end of the summer Marshall had broken ground for the operations on the site, building a cabin, the lumber mill building, and a dam.

On January 24, 1848, Marshall was walking down the ditch admiring his handiwork when he noticed some pieces of yellow flake. He got a tin plate and went to the river to pan the contents. In a short period of time, he had enough color to completely cover a dime. This was very curious. That night he opened the gate on the dam and ran water through the ditch. The next evening he shut off the gate and let the ditch dry out. He again walked down the ditch and found "a piece half the size of a pea." He called his men over and showed them. By now he was getting excited. "My eye was caught by something shining in the bottom of the ditch. I reached my hand down and picked it up. It made my heart thump, for I was certain it was gold."

After collecting his wits, he rode off to Fort Sutter in a pounding rainstorm. Marshall explained the situation to Sutter behind closed doors. He asked if he could test the nuggets and dust. He showed Sutter his poke, pouring out a handful. Sutter suspected it was gold, but he performed several tests to satisfy his curiosity—the chemical and other analyses bore out his supposition.

Several days later Sutter rode out to the mill to take a look at the find for himself. He told the men to keep the discovery private while he considered what to do. On the sly, he went to the local Indians and bought up the land around the mill for practically nothing. He even wrote to Monterey to secure the mineral rights.

A man named Sam Brannan turned the Sutter's Mill find into a media event that helped make the strike big news. Brannan was a clever entrepreneur who knew how to stack the deck so he could make a dollar. With an eye for business, Sam Brannan established a flour mill and started the *California Star*, the first newspaper in San Francisco. When he heard about the gold strike, he planned to capitalize on it. He wasn't interested in picking or panning; he felt the biggest profits could be realized by outfitting and selling to the miners. He knew how important this discovery might be and how much business it could create. Brannan started by opening up a store near Sutter's Mill, which he stocked with foodstuffs, picks, shovels, pans, and other gear a miner would need to ply his trade.

Gold in California was nothing new. Claims had been filed from time to time with success. For example in the Los Angeles area several decades earlier, a notable gold strike was made. On March 15, 1848, the *Californian*, a San Francisco paper, ran "Gold Mine Found" on the back page. The article mentioned how folks at Sutter's Mill were paying for goods with gold dust. There wasn't a lot of excitement . . . yet. For some time, the news about the Sutter's Mill strike stayed regional.

Brannan then did his best to publicize the find. He promoted the discovery in the *Star*, and to stir the pot, he walked through San Francisco waving his hat for folks to gather around. He held up a quinine bottle of nuggets and dust, shouting, "Gold! Gold! Gold! On the American River!" This phrase became the anthem. By June the rush was on in the region. Nearly all of Sutter's workers deserted him to dig for gold. Accounts say that San Francisco nearly became a ghost town. Every man who could wield a shovel or a pick was in the foothills looking to get rich.

In August the military governor, Colonel R. B. Mason, made an official tour of the gold fields. Accompanying him was a young lieutenant named William Tecumseh Sherman. They wrote up an official glowing report to send back to Washington. They also included $3,900 worth of nuggets and dust to punctuate their document. The report also mentioned that more than four thousand men were working the fields, and the number was growing. They suggested that some of the best claims were producing $30,000 to $50,000 a day.

The news was pleasing to President James Polk. In his message to Congress in January of the next year, the president said that these reports "would scarcely command belief were they not corroborated by authentic reports." The president mentioned that the price of the recent Mexican War, California being one of the acquisitions, would be paid for many times over by this gold strike alone. His enthusiasm was infectious. Within a few days, the country was suffering from a severe case of gold fever. No one could talk of anything else. Newspaper headlines told of overnight fortunes. Money was to be made not just in gold but in outfitting the droves of men heading for the gold fields.

Sutter was never able to sell the land he had purchased from the Indians because the region became swamped with so many aspiring miners; claim sales were hopeless. He had no way of enforcing trespassing laws. By the end of the summer, more than ten thousand men were looking for color. San Francisco, temporarily deserted, became a boom town overnight. Even the banks were open twenty-four hours a day. During the summer of 1849, a boarding house might have twenty to a hundred cots in one room. A cot cost twenty dollars a week for an eight-hour shift—a sleeper had to bring his own bedding. A lot in town that sold for twenty-one dollars in 1847 might sell for five to seven thousand dollars by the spring of 1849. By the end of that year, that same lot would sell for thirty to forty thousand dollars. There was no end to the brothels, bars, and gambling establishments to tempt the miners coming to town. In 1847 there were fewer than five hundred people in San Francisco. By 1849 there were at least twenty-five thousand inhabitants.

The strike spread out from Sutter's Mill. Placerville, at first called Dry Digs or Hang Town, was one of the richest strikes in California. It wasn't a safe place to be if you were a foreigner. It got its name Hang Town honestly. Three men of foreign birth were accused of stealing a few items. At first their punishment was thirty lashes, but that wasn't enough to satisfy the miners. Someone suggested hanging. The men were tried, found guilty, and hanged by two hundred miners.

North of Sutter's Mill, the Feather River Canyon also produced a lot of gold. Two mines took out three hundred pounds of nuggets and dust in two weeks. This turned the country upside down. On the North Fork of the Yuba River, some miners stopped to catch some fish before moving on to their area. They boiled their salmon and ate their lunch. When they started to clean up the dishes, they found gold in the bottom of the pot.

The gold strike lasted until the mid-1850s. About $400 million worth of gold found its way to San Francisco, alone. All together about $600 million in gold was taken from the gold fields by 1860. While the California gold strike was probably the most important in the 1800s (after all, it helped define and populate a new state), it wasn't the most lucrative. The famous Nevada Comstock "Lode," alone, located in the Washoe Mountains in 1859, produced more than $400 million in less than thirty years. The Black Hills Homestake Mine discovered in 1876 by Fred and Mose Manuel produced a billion dollars and may be the single richest mine in history. In Deadwood, South Dakota, more than one hundred thousand dollars' worth of gold a day was being transacted. And by 1870 Colorado mines had produced more gold overall than California.

The California strike helped build and populate the West, but like most gold strikes, the real harvest was the richness of the land the miners had overlooked.

Sutter's sawmill circa 1852 (the name of the man is believed to be James Marshall)

THE MOUNTAIN MEADOWS MASSACRE: THE MYSTERY OF A BLOODY MASS MURDER

Did southern Utah settlers encourage the Paiutes to attack the Fancher wagon train? Was John D. Lee the leader of the white murderers? Was the Mormon prophet, Brigham Young, responsible for this massacre?

In southern Utah there is a small, quiet valley known as Mountain Meadows. The nights are cool; the summer grasses wave in the breeze. Seeps and springs provide fresh water. The peaceful surroundings belie the fact that on September 11, 1857, approximately 120 men, women, and children were murdered in cold blood at the site. The tragedy of the Mountain Meadows Massacre has never been fully explained. A century and a half later, there are still more questions than answers.

In the three decades since its humble beginnings in New York, members of the Church of Jesus Christ of Latter-day Saints, the Mormons, had suffered considerable persecution in the East and had been driven west from New York to Ohio and then to Missouri and Illinois by suspicion and prejudice. In Illinois they had created a beautiful city called Nauvoo, which, at the time, was the largest and most affluent township of any in the state (including Chicago).

Mormons, officially called The Church of Jesus Christ of Latter-day Saints, believed a boy prophet, Joseph Smith, had a divine visit and was called to restore Christ's church. They also believed in a translated book of scripture called the Book of Mormon—which they felt complemented the Bible. Other beliefs, such as polygamy and a hatred of slavery, fueled angry pro-slavery mobs near Nauvoo. These men took Joseph Smith, and his brother, Hyrum, and brutally murdered them in nearby Carthage, Illinois. Continued mob violence forced the Mormons to flee to Iowa where, in 1847, Brigham Young organized a mass migration across the Great Plains to the Rocky Mountains. The Mormon people hoped to settle unmolested and make a new life free from persecution in the Great Basin, often called the Great American Desert. There they established an independent republic called Deseret. They considered themselves loyal Americans, but they had an inherent fear and distrust of the government, which had done precious little to protect their civil rights in Missouri, and they wanted to be left alone to practice their religion.

By 1857 the Mormons had carved out settlements in the Great Basin and were prospering. Brigham Young had enjoyed a peaceful tenure as the recognized territorial governor. Then, on July 24, four men rode into Salt Lake with frightful news; a large contingent of the US Army was marching on them.

Democrat James Buchanan had just been elected president of the United States. Buchanan knew that the nation was facing a serious division over the issue of slavery, and he tried to sidestep this by focusing on the Mormons instead. Ironically few, if any, problems had existed between Utah Territory and the United States to this point. The territory was, however, staunchly anti-slavery, which was a thorny issue for the president. An advisor named John Tyler sent a letter to Buchanan that proposed wiping out the Mormon influence in the Utah Territory, a plan that would divorce the Democrats from any association with Mormon philosophy and divert national attention from the issue of slavery. Tyler said, "The popular idea is rapidly maturing that Mormonism . . . should be put down and utterly extirpated. I believe we can supersede the Negro-Mania with the almost universal excitement of an anti-Mormon crusade. Should you . . . seize this question with a strong, fearless and resolute hand, the country I am sure will rally."

Brigham Young, the territorial governor, was replaced by Alfred Cummings. The president, however, didn't bother to tell Governor Young there was going to be a change. Instead he sent a large army to intimidate the church into compliance.

When the Mormon people heard that more than 2,600 well-armed men under the command of Colonel Johnston were marching to Salt Lake City to "whip the Mormons," panic and fear ensued. Painful memories of the persecution they had faced in the east resurfaced. Martial law was enacted, and the Nauvoo Legion was called out for the "Big Fight." Brigham Young and the church leaders advised the Saints (Mormons) that war with the US Army could be at hand.

Brigham Young knew the advancing army depended upon having its supplies replenished when it arrived in Utah and he wasn't going to let that happen. It would be easier to starve an army than fight it. He was prepared to "scorch the earth" if necessary, burning everything in the path of the approaching troops: fields, homes, businesses, and barns. In the meantime the Mormons (along with their supplies and livestock) would retreat south, as necessary, from the encroaching foe.

Brigham told church members to stockpile all surplus supplies, especially food, against the coming war. Precarious times demanded extreme actions. Nothing was to be sold to non-members, especially food, guns, and ammunition.

Indian diplomacy in the Great Basin was a pressing issue that needed immediate attention. Unlike elsewhere in the west, there had been few confrontations with native peoples as Mormons had fanned out into many parts of the Great Basin. Brigham's philosophy was "it's easier to feed 'em than fight 'em." Nevertheless as the settlers needed more land to make a living, Native Americans in the region understandably felt they were being pushed out of their traditional homelands.

In southern Utah Territory, Indians still outnumbered white settlers five to one. It was the church's plan to keep the tribes neutral—or better, on the Mormons' side in the conflict with the government. Their plan was to appease the tribes at all costs so a peace could be maintained. Jacob Hamblin was the Mormon in charge of the southern Indian tribes. He gathered twelve chiefs among the Paiutes, Pahvants, and Utes for a parley.

While the Great Basin was stirring with anxiety, a group of settlers left Arkansas later in the season than was prudent. The Fancher party planned to travel overland to California via Salt Lake City. With more than forty wagons, carriages, hundreds of horses, and perhaps a thousand head of cattle, they thought they were well-prepared for the long trip.

They made good time, but after crossing the Rockies, the party was understandably worried about the Sierra Nevada. An early snowfall would make the mountains impassable. By August they had reached Emigration Canyon outside of Salt Lake. At first they decided to make a fast dash for Donner Pass in the Sierra Nevada. While it was the most direct route, it was also the most treacherous. The Sierras were unforgiving—and the fact that the Donner party had recently met with tragedy was no doubt weighing heavily on their minds. A few days out of Salt Lake, however, the Fancher party decided to turn around. The party leaders felt it would be best to follow the southern route, which would take them through the heart of the Great Basin and on to Los Angeles. This detour was longer, but it would be an easier trip and the mountain passes going to southern California were considerably lower. Furthermore the party was running dangerously short of supplies, and they thought they could replenish them in Salt Lake. However when the Fancher party got to Salt Lake, they were angered to find most of the stores boarded up. The supplies they needed had been stockpiled against the expected "Utah" war and were not for sale. This didn't help the mood of the party. Local residents would say that the Fancher party was "rude, defiant, and boisterous." As events played out, the story of the encounters with the Fanchers became increasingly muddled.

The wagon train moved south, hoping to buy supplies farther along the route. Captain Fancher, however, and some of the men, didn't win many friends among the Latter-day Saints. They bragged about driving the Mormons out of Missouri, about being at the Carthage jail in Illinois to help kill Joseph Smith, and about killing Mormons. Stories also circulated that one Fancher man bragged that he had the pistol that had killed Joseph and Hyrum Smith. Some of the men in the party snapped the heads off chickens with their bullwhips and grazed their animals, which were considerable, in fields that were ready to be harvested. If these stories were true, or even if the locals only believed them to be true, it's easy to see why the Mormon merchants wouldn't go out of their way to sell the party what it needed. The unwritten code of the West meant that people helped each other. When you came to a town, ranch, or settlement, you could expect to graze and water your stock, rest in the shade, and likely share a meal. Friendly conversation with travelers and emigrants was how Western folks stayed current on news and gossip. The Mormon people, in particular, were noted for their kindness to travelers, especially in rural areas. But it appears that at this worst of times, the Fancher party may have continually violated this unwritten code.

In Fillmore they tried again to get supplies without success. After a layover at Corn Creek, they proceeded to Beaver and again their attempts were unsuccessful. Outside of Parowan, the party may have had an abusive encounter with members of the Paiute tribe. There is some confusion about what they did or didn't do. They might have poisoned a waterhole that caused the death of several tribal members and some livestock. In an emotionally charged environment, they angered not only the Mormons but also the local Indians.

Mormon John D. Lee was quickly dispatched to talk to the Paiutes, who were reportedly ready to attack the wagon train. He told local leaders that the Indians felt they had been insulted. Some of the brethren on the High Council wanted to confront the wagon train directly. Others suggested they send a message to church headquarters to find out what Brigham Young wanted them to do. James Haslam left immediately on a fast horse with a letter to Brigham Young. However, with the rough condition of the roads, it would take at least six or seven days for a return message.

Meanwhile, a frustrated Captain Fancher led his wagons out of Cedar City to Mountain Meadows, thirty miles southwest of Cedar City, a traditional stopping place on the Old Spanish Trail. There was good water and grass, so they could rest their livestock before the four-thousand-foot drop to the desert floor where, this late in the year, water and feed would be sparse. Getting the stock in good shape for the desert journey was critical. And they were still short on supplies.

Paiute scouts had been trailing the train since Fillmore and, apparently, had been sending back reports to the chiefs. When the Fancher party stopped to rest in Mountain Meadows, they were attacked. The Fancher party was fairly experienced; these men and women were veterans of the trail. They quickly formed the wagons into a circle, mounted breastworks, and fought bravely, although they soon ran short of powder and lead. After the first day, a handful of men were killed, another handful wounded. The siege went on for a few days and two Paiute chiefs were killed.

What happened next is one of the bigger mysteries of the West. Because the Paiutes' assaults were apparently unsuccessful, some apologists have suggested that Native American warriors demanded help from the Utah settlers in destroying the wagon train. There is evidence that they threatened to unleash their collective fury upon the settlers' farms and towns if they didn't get cooperation. The Paiutes greatly outnumbered the Mormons, who felt it necessary to do anything to keep the peace.

Other historians think that John D. Lee, under the direction of the Cedar City High Council, had encouraged the major Paiute chiefs—Jackson, Tatse-gibbits, Big-Bill, Moqueetus, Young-quick, and Nou-cop—to attack the train. It is also conceivable that John D. Lee may have tried to talk the chiefs out of war but wasn't successful. Even if they weren't directly involved, the local Mormon leaders must have known after a few days that the warriors had not successfully wiped out the Fancher party, and their two Paiute chiefs had been killed. Possibly some local officials might even have felt that as long as the fighting was done by the hostiles, their hands would be clean and the problem wagon train would be dealt with. While we don't know the details, local Mormon leaders felt the situation had become tenuous. To protect themselves, they activated the Iron County Militia under Colonel William H. Dane while they awaited word from Salt Lake. After three days of fighting, on September 9, three Fancher men slipped out in desperation and tried to go for help in Cedar City. All three men were killed—two shot by Mormon militia guards.

We assume that local church leaders may have felt the death of these men tangled matters. If word got out that the Mormons had killed members of the wagon train, even by accident, it could bring retribution down upon the people because the federal army would surely seek revenge.

The militia rode to Mountain Meadows. Perhaps it was to help the Fancher party; perhaps it was to help the Paiutes wipe out the wagon train. Nevertheless, things got out of hand and what happened next was unconscionable. Under a flag of truce, John D. Lee rode down to the battle-weary wagons. One version of the story says that Lee talked to the pioneers and told them that he could convince the Indians to let the party go, if they would leave their wagons and supplies and walk out. To come this far and lose all their worldly goods to Indians—and in the heart of Mormon territory—would have been a bitter pill to swallow. But the story goes that Lee convinced the emigrants that the Paiutes were only after their possessions and that they could escape with their lives if they left immediately. Apparently they capitulated, having no other choice. The youngest children were sent ahead in a wagon. The wounded were loaded into another wagon.

Lee may have then told the emigrants that they should walk in single file—possibly between militiamen—for their safety. Soon after, according to legend, someone said, "Do your duty," at which point, the militia, possibly with the help of the Paiutes, turned and shot the settlers in cold blood.

Later, Lee claimed his orders were "that the emigrants must be done away with." He also said that when he read his orders, he was so upset that he wadded them up and threw them down. He continued by suggesting he was supposed to "decoy the emigrants from their position and kill all that could talk. This was the order in writing and I read it."

Another Mormon militia member, John Higbee, testified that the orders said they were *not* to fight "while there is an army marching against our people." Higbee further suggested he had told Lee he hoped to control the Indians so he could save the people.

But "eyewitness" accounts differ. Another version of the story has fewer men escorting the beaten Fancher party. When the command was given, probably at a prescribed spot, where they were flanked by scrub oak and brush on each side, the accompanying militia jumped into the brush where their compatriots were hiding. From this vantage they fired upon the helpless pioneers. More shocking, some of the current archeological evidence from the site indicates that the party might have been shot in the backs of their heads execution-style (while kneeling).

On September 13, Brigham Young's message arrived in Cedar City in record time. It read, "In regard to the emigration trains passing through our settlements, we must not interfere. . . . You must not meddle with them. There are no other trains that I know of. Let them go in peace." When Isaac Haight read the letter from the prophet, he is supposed to have cried and said, "Too late, too late!"

Between 95 and 120 people were massacred that day at Mountain Meadows. We're not sure about the exact number because we don't know positively how many were killed in the previous Indian attacks—or even for certain if there were previous attacks. All of the children from the wagon train under age seven were adopted into local families. Several years later Congress mandated that they be returned to their relatives in Arkansas. John D. Lee is supposed to have reported to Brigham Young that the massacre was committed by Paiutes, and that the settlers weren't responsible for the bloody act. Isaac Haight is thought to have talked to Brigham Young, too, and corroborated Lee's account of an Indian massacre. The men involved may have taken an oath that they would not talk about what they had done or what had actually happened.

But, before long, rumors started to slip out and eventually, there was an official investigation led by Jacob Forney, superintendent of Indian Affairs. John D. Lee caught most of the blame for the crime. He proclaimed his innocence, saying he did not know what was going to happen and suggested that he was leading the party out of the valley and was well in front of the group when he heard the command to shoot. The first time he was tried in a court of law, the jury was hung. The second time, he was found guilty. Judge John Cradlebaugh pronounced the death sentence. On March 23, 1877, Lee was executed at the scene of the crime by a firing squad. It's hard to imagine Isaac Haight, Colonel William H. Dane, and John M. Higbee not sharing the blame. Whether or not Brigham Young was complicit in the tragedy has also been a matter of some debate.

Few records of the tragedy remain because those who were involved cloaked themselves in secrecy. As time passes we continue to unearth pieces of this puzzle, but it's not enough to give us a clear picture. The anxiety and fear felt by the Mormon people during the summer of 1857 was real, and what happened was most likely the result of good men, afraid and worried about a larger situation, getting carried away. Panic compounded the problem until things were out of control and they seduced themselves into committing a horrific mass murder for the good of their community, the good of their settlement, and the good of their church.

Although it is fairly clear that the local Mormon settlers were in some way responsible for the tragedy, no one knows for certain how far the church's culpability stretches. Some historians have suggested that Brigham Young was essentially responsible, implying that the southern Utah settlers were simply acting under his direction, but the evidence does not indicate that the Mormon prophet knew about what was occurring before the fact. There was no train or telegraph at that time between the two communities. It was a six-hundred-mile round trip between southern Utah and Salt Lake City on bad roads. A coordinated effort to plan the demise of the train was unlikely, if not impossible. In addition, the Mormon people had always been quite passive and nonviolent. They were pushed from New York to Ohio, Missouri, Illinois, Iowa, and finally Utah without a fight.

John D. Lee

When Joseph Smith was murdered in Carthage, they mourned their fallen leader and allowed themselves to be displaced.

Mountain Meadows remains a black mark in the history of the American West, and the controversy surrounding what really happened that day will never be fully understood.

GEORGE ARMSTRONG CUSTER: RISKING HIS CAREER TO DEFEND INDIAN RIGHTS

Was General George Armstrong Custer as flamboyant, arrogant, and one-dimensional as history has portrayed him? Was Custer, Civil War hero and plains cavalryman, a defender of the Indians? Was there another side to Custer that we sometimes neglect?

General George Armstrong Custer loved the limelight. He was also a man of apparent contradictions—generous to a fault on one occasion yet petty on another. Driven to seek wealth, he often fell into disastrous get-rich-quick schemes. He could weep openly, unashamedly, over the loss of a favorite dog or a sad scene in a play yet laugh almost uncontrollably over something that struck him funny. He could kill a man without a second's regret, but was willing to risk his life to save a stray animal. At times the general could be a pompous ass, as pretentious and flamboyant as a modern-day rock star. He was especially vain about his clothing and appearance—even in the field. Custer, it appears, was fated either to be loved or hated by his men, his superiors, and posterity. General Ulysses S. Grant, later President Grant, his commanding officer, referred to him as "a strutting peacock."

No one, however, not even his harshest critics, questioned his valor on the field or the accolades he won during the Civil War. The press called him "the boy general" since he was the youngest officer in US history to earn this prestigious brevet field rank. This was quite an accomplishment for a cadet who graduated last in his class at West Point. In battle he earned a reputation for being a gallant, if not reckless, warrior. He was also known as a zealous Indian fighter and shameless self-promoter.

What many don't know is that George Armstrong Custer, Civil War hero, Indian fighter and butcher, ironically had a great respect for Native Americans, especially the Plains tribes. On occasion he was their outspoken defender. Courageously he put his rising military career in serious jeopardy when he exposed the rampant corruption so prevalent both in Washington and on the frontier. In the 1870s, defending the "savage" Indian publicly, especially for an army officer, was not prudent. General Phil Sheridan summed up the feelings of most people when he said, "The only good Indians I ever saw were dead." Nevertheless, Custer, the flamboyant iconoclast, blew the whistle and caught the attention of the Eastern press. He violated the unwritten code of a US Army officer, speaking against his military and political leaders (especially his commander-in-chief), and was immediately relieved of his command.

As out of character as it might seem for a man known as an Indian fighter, George Armstrong "Autie" Custer had a soft spot for the "hostiles." His admiration certainly didn't keep him from making war, nor on occasion from ruthlessly wiping out a settlement or two that got in his way, but he had an appreciation, if not a fascination, for Indians and admired their way of life. Custer never lost his boyish enthusiasm or the accompanying romanticism that came from reading too many adventure novels.

He viewed the Native Americans as "noble savages," even if, sadly, the white man was the superior, inevitable conqueror. He felt war was a glorious adventure. On one occasion, he told a superior that he could easily be an Indian—and he meant it. He said if he were an Indian, he'd be with the free-roaming tribes, fighting to the death before submitting to the tame way of life. Custer was understandably appalled with the way Native Americans were treated on reservations. "Contained" Indians who no longer followed the game herds were at the mercy of unscrupulous agents and dishonest government officials. Government handouts to the reservations were often moldy and rotten, thanks to corrupt agents who got rich while their charges starved. He was also aware of how government officials had broken their word. He felt that if the government was going to keep tribes on reservations, it needed a fair, consistent policy for better treatment—and honest men to oversee it.

Custer, like his superiors Generals Sheridan and Sherman, argued that the Bureau of Indian Affairs, which was currently under the Department of the Interior, should be transferred to the War Department (as it had been prior to 1849). The soldiers were only too aware that Indian Affairs was slippery and corrupt, causing more problems than it solved. If the agency was under the auspices of the War Department (which was far less corrupt), then the problems could be more quickly contained. Unquestionably a starving Indian was more likely to break loose from the reservation and cause problems. Who could blame warriors for trying to feed their families? The army knew that it was in everyone's best interest to keep the tribes fed.

In the winter of 1875 and 1876, George and Elizabeth "Libby" Custer spent four months vacationing in the East. They visited friends, ate fancy dinners, attended parties, and went to the theater. George was something of a celebrity, a status he enjoyed and perpetuated. His military activities, as well as his books and adventure articles, helped keep him in the public eye. At one point he and his wife entertained an offer from the Redpath Lyceum Bureau to go on the lecture circuit for $250 a presentation. This was a considerable amount of money so the offer was tempting, but Custer reluctantly turned it down. He knew he'd be involved in a major campaign the next summer and felt the notoriety from this endeavor, which would be heavily covered by the press, might catapult him into national office. Furthermore Custer loved the excitement of the chase and knew he wasn't yet ready to lead a more genteel life.

In March of 1876, barely home from vacation, Custer got a telegraph from Washington, DC. He was summoned by Representative Heister Clymer to appear before the House Committee on Expenditures. He got permission from his superiors and started packing for the weeklong trip to the capital. On March 21 he left Fort Abraham Lincoln by horse-drawn sled for the train station.

Custer knew the "loyal" opposition was anxious to expose scandal in the Grant Administration. The Democrats were looking toward the next election and wanted to see President Grant replaced. On the sly, Custer had sent "dirt" about the current administration's shortcomings to reporter friends working for anti-Grant publications. He trusted his name would never be mentioned, but any muck Democrats could rake up and publish would help in the next presidential bid. For some time Representative Clymer had been investigating Secretary of War Belknap on charges of corruption relating to post traderships. Evidence mounted and under pressure, Belknap tendered his resignation on March 2; the president "reluctantly" accepted it.

President Grant hoped the resignation of his secretary of war would reduce the political pressures he was feeling. If anything, though, it chummed his adversaries to heightened frenzies while they looked for further malfeasance. Clymer renewed his attacks with a vengeance, hoping to capture more Grant officials in his net and continue to embarrass the president's administration; like others in his party, he hoped the negative publicity would reduce the Republican party's chances, specifically Grant's, for a third term. While the merits of Ulysses S. Grant as a general can be argued, there was little doubt that Grant was a poor president. He had an unfortunate flair for appointing opportunistic, corrupt officials who bilked their offices for personal gain. Most agree that Grant was a decent man, but he was ill-suited for the highest office in the land. He was elected because of his service record; indeed Grant was one of the most popular men in the country. Some historians have called him a "puritan in Babylon."

The more Clymer dug, the more corruption he found. Calling Custer to testify before the committee was a politically astute move for Clymer. The general had been critical of Indian policies for years. And Clymer knew for some time that George Custer had done more than supply "muck" to reporter friends, he had personally penned critical pieces about Grant Administration policies under a pseudonym. On their trips to the East, Custer and his wife were careful to make "connections" with important Democrats. Custer secretly hoped that he might be drafted as a candidate for the fall presidential election, which is why the ensuing notoriety from the summer campaign was so important to him. At the least, if Grant was defeated, he could expect to be made a brigadier general under a new president. It was no secret that he was a confirmed Democrat with political aspirations. As an expert on Indian affairs—specifically Indian and reservation policy, Indian agents and traders, and the consequences of government graft—he was an ideal witness. Before he left, Libby, knowing his disposition, warned him to "avoid politics" for the time being. To no one's surprise, however, he rushed headfirst into this political battle.

Before he testified, he had dinners and meetings with Representative Clymer, among other important party leaders. He wanted them to know he was a man to be reckoned with. He was not a hostile witness by any stretch of the imagination, so the Democrats got an early Christmas present. On April 18, he came before the committee on Indian Affairs. Custer did more than answer the posed questions; he elaborated in great detail. A good portion of his testimony was first-hand observations of the inequities he had experienced after ten years on the Plains. He was blunt and direct. Other parts of his testimony were damning, even though partly based on hearsay. He didn't fail to mention names, either. He blasted former Secretary of War Belknap. He also implicated Orville Grant, the president's brother, whom he said, like Belknap, shared in the corrupt profits at the expense of native peoples.

The political fallout for President Grant was immense. "The press is eating me alive," he claimed. Grant was livid that one of his officers would say such slander. On April 20, Custer left Washington for his regiment but was called back. Grant couldn't erase Custer's testimony, but he could relieve him of his command. A shattered Custer tried and tried to meet with his commander-in-chief, but the president would not see him. General Custer again appealed to his superiors, Generals Sherman and Sheridan, close personal friends of the president who had saved Custer in the past. He also appealed to his friend and superior General Alfred Terry. Through Terry, he wrote a note to the President: "I appeal to you as a soldier to spare me the humiliation of seeing my regiment march to meet the enemy and I not share its dangers."

Finally Grant capitulated to the press, and more importantly to his generals, and reinstated Custer—but not without "clipping the peacock's wings." Grant refused to let him lead the summer campaign as previously planned. This responsibility would now fall upon General Terry. Custer's activities would be somewhat limited.

It is correct to assume that some of what Custer said before the committee was politically motivated. He did aspire to political office, or at least military advancement. But it would be wrong to think he acted out of purely calculated political motives. The general didn't think things through that carefully. In the recent Civil War, he'd led a number of dangerous charges against the enemy—having at least eleven horses shot out from under him. He saw an enemy and charged; he didn't plan stratagems. He was always at the front, the vanguard, of any endeavor he was involved in. Like a yellow-haired Don Quixote, he was always in the lead, bullets whizzing about his head, reckless and determined, certain that God, truth, and righteousness were on his side. He never looked back.

His behavior before the committee was predictable. He wasn't capable of dancing around an issue. Custer saw the enemy, which in this case was ambiguous policy and corruption, and charged headfirst. A frontal assault, no matter what the personal risks, had always served him. Life for Autie Custer was black and white—he was a player in a storybook.

Custer-bashing has been fashionable since the 1960s, but the truth is the boy general didn't die for our nation's collective sins—he was simply an instrument. President Grant, General Sherman, and General Sheridan are far more culpable. Moral deconstruction of our history, after all, is a luxury granted to winners who feel the pricks of morning-after social consciousness. The boy general was a well-dressed racial scalpel employed by chess players in a utilitarian game of manifest destiny. Like the buffalo, the carrier pigeon, or the grizzly bear, George Armstrong Custer, too, became a symbol of the passing frontier and the price, the sacrifice, one must pay to tame the West. The price was not cheap.

Custer campaigns were always violent and bloody and the body count was always high (the Washita comes to mind) *which is the point*. Custer spin made good headlines for an Eastern press. We must keep in mind that he was a soldier following orders from superior officers who knew *exactly* what he would do. Custer was the fated hero who would not live long enough to confront his tragic flaws. Custer's war talents for the Sioux Campaign were as critical as Achilles' talents for the *Iliad* . . . and the commanding generals knew it. Neither Custer nor Achilles, of course, lived long enough to understand the dystopia created by their actions or the effects on the enemy. They died as legends to be shaped by future generations.

General George Armstrong Custer

Custer was no more or less "brutal" or "bloody" with the hostiles than other commanding officers history has chosen to let rest in peace. It is ironic that unlike most of his associates, Custer advocated humane and fair treatment for his "enemy" after they were brought into submission. To his credit, he spoke for the Sioux in a time when many considered the indigenous peoples vermin.

Nowadays we take comfort in blaming Custer for the nation's treatment of Native Americans. He paid a price for his personal and professional hubris at the Little Bighorn, but culpability more correctly rests with decades of carelessly designed Indian policies and national attitudes about indigenous people. Blame also rests with a government that subscribed to the thesis that men were created equal but debated whether or not Native Americans (or blacks) had souls or were even human. Censure rests with an expanding nation that coveted "promised" lands and additional natural resources, so it broke its word for political expediency and gold.

For seventy-five years after his death, the general was looked upon as some sort of holy "frontier" martyr. The public, with the help of his widow, put him on a pedestal and held him up as a paragon of all that was good and right. Even Teddy Roosevelt lauded him and called him an example for young children everywhere. In modern times, however, Custer's stock is at an all time low. Nowadays he has come to represent all that was wrong with the Western movement. This, of course, is as wrong as making him into an idol.

Perhaps it's time to take the general out, dust him off, and put him in his rightful place. George Armstrong Custer wasn't a saint, he was a tool.

SITTING BULL: HIS ROLE AT THE BATTLE OF THE LITTLE BIGHORN

What was Sitting Bull's role in the Battle of the Little Bighorn? Did he take an active role in the fighting and kill Custer as some legends claim, or was he hiding? And, why has this chief been such a lightning rod for the last 125 years?

After the June 1876 Battle of the Little Bighorn, Americans didn't know what to think. How could the flamboyant Custer, the war hero who had become a brevet major general at age twenty-three during the Civil War, the darling Indian fighter of the Plains, lie dead, mutilated, and bloated with his beloved Seventh Cavalry on some obscure Montana slope? Americans wondered how a band of Indians could defeat one of the best equipped, and supposedly best led, modern armies in the world. The country was in a state of shock. The American public clamored to know what really happened on that hot, fateful day in late June when the Sioux Nation triumphed against the cavalry.

The Battle of the Little Bighorn was arguably the most significant Native American victory in history. The humiliating massacre stung smartly, wounding the national ego, and hastened the inevitable destruction of the Plains tribes. The Indians were summarily hounded to capitulation by a relentless army with a vendetta, an army representing the will of the people. While the Sioux, along with their Northern Cheyenne allies, had certainly won the battle (as well as the Battle of the Rosebud against General Crook a few days earlier), they lost the war. Within a few short years, a traditional way of life, along with the buffalo herds, was just a memory.

Sitting Bull, the great Sioux warrior and holy man, was one of the most important chiefs in our nation's history. Not only was he the leader of his band, the Hunkpapa, he was the first chief elected to represent all the free-roaming Sioux (sometimes referred to as the Teton Sioux). These tribes included the Hunkpapa, Blackfoot, Brule, Two Kettles, Oglala, Minneconjou, and Sans Arc. Making Sitting Bull their leader was an act of supreme confidence for a people who cherished personal and tribal autonomy above all else.

After his Sioux warriors defeated Custer's cavalry, Sitting Bull became the whipping boy for the country's accumulated frustrations. Ridiculous stories circulated in the press to help explain how such a catastrophe had occurred. Some thought it impossible that an "unlearned savage" could defeat one of West Point's finest—never mind that the "finest" graduated last in his class. Some journalists suggested that Sitting Bull surely must have attended West Point incognito where he'd learned military tactics to help him outwit the US Army. Other observers wondered if this heathen prodigy had somehow been trained in Europe before returning to lead his tribe. There was speculation that the chief might have learned to read English, French, and even Latin from missionaries and thus studied books on military maneuvers in his teepee by firelight. How else could he defeat the US Cavalry?

In addition to discussions of his training as a battlefield tactician, there was speculation about how Sitting Bull actually commanded his men during Custer's Last Stand. Some argued that Sitting Bull was at the head of his braves, personally leading wave after wave against the gallant boys in blue. Others suggested he wasn't fighting at all. Rather he was hung over, scared, and/or hiding. They argued that his braves, because of their overwhelming numbers, won the field; it had nothing to do with his leadership, even though Sitting Bull took credit for the victory.

James McLaughlin, who was the agent at the Standing Rock Agency (a precursor to what we today call a reservation) from 1881 to 1895 and no friend of Sitting Bull, felt that the chief was "a physical coward." Agent McLaughlin suggested that as soon as the first bullets started to fly through the teepees at the start of the battle, the chief "felt panic in his heart," collected his wives, and took off to the west like a frightened cottontail rabbit. McLaughlin claimed that Sioux scouts found Sitting Bull after he was about ten miles out, and informed him that Long Hair (the Sioux name for Custer) was defeated. He returned and claimed the victory. McLaughlin was not anywhere near the battlefield so his comments must be taken in their context; nevertheless, they reflected contemporary thinking.

Much of what was written in the late 1800s is, at best, of uncertain origin. To further justify and explain the defeat, nineteenth-century critics often inflated the number of Indians in the battle, making the defeat a little more bearable to a wondering nation. It wasn't so ignominious a slaughter if the poor troopers were grossly outnumbered ten-, twenty-, or thirty-to-one. Even Henry Wadsworth Longfellow couldn't resist getting into the act. Longfellow, the most widely read American poet of his day, had Sitting Bull cleverly waiting in ambush and mounting an attack with three thousand braves. Never mind that the Seventh attacked the Sioux camp first. His sentimental poem about the Little Bighorn, no doubt written in a moment of frenetic national patriotism, takes a great deal of poetic license. Today, his factual errors are laughable, but in his time the poem was taken as gospel.

It's not surprising that a great deal of the fiction surrounding Sitting Bull and the Battle of the Little Bighorn was carried into the twentieth century. The real Sitting Bull was indeed enigmatic, but there are also a number of facts about this fascinating leader buried under more than a hundred years of myth and prejudice.

In order to understand Sitting Bull, as a political figure and a man, we must understand the events that were affecting his people. As the insightful historian Robert Utely has commented, Sitting Bull viewed himself foremost as his people's lance and shield in a confusing, threatening time. As a warrior, and later as a chief, Sitting Bull exemplified all the cardinal virtues of his religion. These included bravery, fortitude (enduring pain and showing dignity when enduring pain), generosity, and wisdom. That Sitting Bull was brave is a matter of record. He had more than sixty-three documented coups, and his prowess as a warrior among his people was legendary.

On one occasion, to show his medicine was strong during a heated battle with the blue coats, Sitting Bull invited several warriors to smoke with him in the face of death. Taking his pipe and tobacco pouch, he walked directly into the line of fire, bullets flying by him. He sat on the ground, lit his pipe, and passed it to some understandably nervous associates—all the while bullets whizzed about the smokers' heads. Finally he tapped out the burnt tobacco and carefully cleaned the bowl with a twig. While the other braves ran back to where the Sioux had taken shelter, Sitting Bull calmly stood up and sauntered to his people, heavy-caliber slugs kicking up dust about him.

Wounded on a number of occasions, he endured without complaint. He was also a frequent participant in the religious Sun Dance ceremony in which braves endured self-torture to earn the favor of the gods. He was selfless and generous to a fault, giving away his possessions and sharing his food with any who were hungry or needy. After the Battle of Powder River on March 17, 1876, the Northern Cheyenne had lost most of their possessions, including their food caches, lodges, and bedding. When the destitute band arrived at Sitting Bull's camp, he had a number of lodges prepared for the cold, starving people. Pot after pot of meat was put on to boil so there would be a great welcoming feast. Then, under his instructions, the Sioux replenished the Cheyenne by giving them presents. They were welcome for as long as they wished to stay. A Cheyenne chief named Wooden Leg said, "Oh what a heart. I will never forget Sitting Bull."

He was the first and the last leader of the free-roaming Sioux tribes. He fought unceasingly for his homeland and was dedicated to the preservation of his people's traditional way of life. He fought against the rising tide of white encroachment.

He never understood how Spotted Tail and Red Cloud could sell out to the whites and take up reservation living, viewing them as traitors to the cause. He refused "to touch the pen to the paper," agreeing with Crazy Horse that "one does not sell the land upon which the people live." He taught that his Sioux should avoid the white man's goods and live in the traditional way. As a brave and a chief he was offended by the string of broken promises and only wanted to live how his fathers had lived, following the buffalo herds. Finally, when he was forced to surrender, as a point of pride, he would not personally hand over his weapon. Instead he handed his rifle to a young boy who in turn gave it to the blue-coat chief.

Sitting Bull was probably born around 1831, close to the Missouri River, most likely near Many Caches. He hunted his first buffalo at the tender age of ten and counted coup in a heated battle with a Crow brave when he was fourteen. He was known as Slow or Jumping Badger. As a young man, he was commended for his bravery in battle and was honored for his generosity, key virtues for a Sioux warrior. He was always at the front of the fighting, risking his life for the defense of his people and for a warrior's glory. Around 1857 he took his father's name and became known as Sitting Bull. His father took a new name.

He fought the western expansion, which threatened the life-giving buffalo herds. By the early 1870s the Sioux were furious at how often the United States government had broken its word. Each year brought more and more white men. The Treaty of 1868, after all, had promised an "unceded territory," a land free of white men where they might live, west of the Missouri River. The land included the Black Hills, which the Sioux considered holy. At the same time a "Great Sioux Reservation" was also created in southwestern South Dakota for the Sioux tribes who had given up the traditional, nomadic life. A good number of the Sioux, perhaps fifteen to eighteen thousand, were lured to agency or reservation living, drawing food rations and other supplies.

The treaty was made worthless when thousands of miners invaded the sacred Black Hills in 1874, ripping up the land looking for gold, logging timber, damming streams, making roads, and building towns. Sitting Bull's people called the thoroughfare entering into the region the Thieves Road. It brought miners, ranchers, farmers, and tradesmen—white men who had come to stay. The tribes also hated the "iron horse," the Northern Pacific Railway, which reached the Missouri by 1873 and was moving toward Yellowstone. Most troubling was the serious reduction in the buffalo herds, the life-blood of the tribe's existence. Buffalo had once covered the plains; now they were fewer and fewer each year, thanks to the white man.

As Sitting Bull had foretold, reservation life wasn't what the white men said it would be. Often the land was ill-suited for crops. Many braves, who had been hunters and warriors, found the life of a farmer degrading and boring. Furthermore the promised supplies and goods were inconsistent and of inferior quality, if they arrived at all. In spite of the army's efforts, disillusioned and hungry agency Indians would slip off the reservation, joining their free-roaming brethren. They wanted to taste buffalo and once again ride their ponies across the prairies as free men. Who would know if they took a few supplies from the Great Father and slipped back to the unceded lands? Each spring the numbers on the reservations diminished. Each fall before the snow flew, the numbers swelled. This was a source of contention for the whites, but there wasn't much they could do at that time.

In 1875 under the direction of President Grant, General Sherman, and General Sheridan, the US Army decided to make one giant military push to finally bring the free-roaming tribes into submission. They were aware that the United States had broken the treaty on a number of occasions; however, that didn't matter. They argued that the free-roaming Sioux had sent war parties around the edges of the unceded lands and had committed acts of hostility, which made it necessary to make war in return. Most importantly, there was so much political pressure to colonize the Black Hills it would be political suicide to let the Sioux keep it. They created the Allison Commission to talk to the tribes, agree upon a price, and purchase the Black Hills. More than four hundred Indians showed up at the conference, but many of the free-roaming chiefs—Sitting Bull and Crazy Horse, most notably—were absent. It was also rumored among the Sioux that Little-Big-Man, a friend of Crazy Horse, would kill anyone who capitulated. The conference did little more than give false legitimacy to the impending action.

Washington then proclaimed that any Indian not on the reservation by January 31, 1876, would be considered hostile and dealt with accordingly. Essentially this edict meant that the United States could do battle legally, if not morally, with tribes that were living on the lands the government had previously promised them. Never mind that it would be nearly impossible to get this mandate out to the free-roaming tribes during the winter months.

In the late spring of 1876, General Terry and General Crook, under the direction of President Grant and Generals Sherman and Sheridan, set out to crush the "offending" Indians once and for all and make the Black Hills "safe for democracy."

General Custer, who was being punished for speaking out against President Grant's Indian policy, nearly missed the big party.

However, at the last minute, thanks to the intervention of Sherman and Sheridan, Custer was assigned to General Terry, albeit in a subordinate role.

The army's approach was a cause for concern to the Sioux. It didn't take a soothsayer to tell them that their homeland was being invaded. With the buffalo vanishing and the Black Hills raped, this intrusion was something that could not be tolerated. They felt, understandably, threatened, although for the moment somewhat secure in their large numbers, since the tribes were still united for the traditional summer gathering. The US Army didn't realize it was about to stumble into one of the largest gatherings of Plains Indians in history.

Most of the year the tribes were broken down into smaller, more manageable bands. This made it easier to follow game herds and to find grass for their ponies, water, and firewood. But in early summer the Sioux, along with their Northern Cheyenne and a few Arapaho allies, met for an annual celebration. This was a time of family reunions, renewing friendships, weddings, and buffalo hunting. Most important, however, it was also the time for the annual Sun Dance and other religious ceremonies. The celebration usually lasted a couple of weeks with the tribes camping in the rich river valleys. Since grass for their numerous ponies, firewood, and water were critical, the group might move every four or five days, perhaps up or down the valley or to another location. Braves went on extended hunting parties. There were feasts and a general family reunion atmosphere. This year, the tribes stayed together longer than usual, knowing there was safety in numbers with so many soldiers on the loose. Additionally, their numbers had swollen because all the hunting parties had returned and, most important, the reservation Indians joining the free-roaming tribes had arrived. The population doubled.

Custer felt comfortable with the Seventh's forces, around 566 enlisted men, thirty-one officers, and thirty-five Indian scouts. This was a more than adequate complement for anything he'd experienced on the Plains thus far. He'd once boasted that with the Seventh he could lick the entire Sioux nation. Surely he thought he'd be fighting one band at a time. Sioux nationalism, a uniting of the tribes, was a new concept (for the Sioux and the US Army). Custer had never encountered a group as large as the one he'd find that decisive June day. Just before attacking, he divided his command into three parts. He rallied the companies he kept with him and charged the Indian camp—not knowing what sort of a hornet's nest he was stepping into.

Even the confident Custer might have done things differently if he had known what he was up against. His scouts had tried to tell him how large this group of Indians was, but he ignored them. Custer knew best. When the general finally realized his mistake, he must have been shocked. There were more than a thousand lodges. This would make the population of the camp more than seven thousand, with arguably fifteen hundred to two thousand warriors. The soldiers were outnumbered roughly three-to-one as they attacked the Sioux.

Wars among the Plains Indians were based on a loose set of prescribed rules that mostly celebrated an individual's efforts of bravery, stealing horses, and counting coup. Doing war with traditional enemies, the hated Crows for example, didn't affect the collective survival of a tribe. War with the *wasichus* (whites) was different. Here was an invading hostile force. The braves weren't fighting just for honor; braves were fighting to save their homeland, their women, and children. Their sacred camp circle had been invaded.

We know from numerous tribal accounts that Sitting Bull had foreseen the attack on his people. In May of 1876, before the grass was fully ripe and the free-roaming tribes met for the annual Sun Dance ceremony, Sitting Bull, the great Sioux prophet, a veteran of many visions, retired to a high bluff to pray to *Wakantanka*, the Sioux god. In his pictorial history, composed years later, he tells how he fell into a trance and saw a great vision: a fantastic dust storm blown frenetically by the eastern wind. He also saw clouds that looked like the lodges or teepees of his people; they were pitched in the valley at the knees of snowy peaks. The dust storm was blown at the lodges with great force. The dust storm was comprised of blue-coated pony soldiers. He could see the stripes on their pants and the guns they carried, the sun reflecting off the barrels, and noted that many of the soldiers were coming upside down. There was thunder and lightning as the two clashed. Finally the dust storm and the soldiers were gone, but the lodges of the people remained.

Sitting Bull came down from the mountain after his experience. He understood his vision and the significance of it, so he gathered the other holy men and war leaders and interpreted his dream. The cloud lodges were the people, the Sioux. The blue coats were the soldiers coming to make war. The Sioux must be ready, and they would win the battle. Sitting Bull knew this because so many soldiers were riding upside down and they had no ears, which meant they would be killed by his people.

To show his faith in his god and to thank the Great Spirit, Sitting Bull vowed "to give flesh" to Wakantanka during the coming

Sun Dance. He also promised a whole buffalo carcass to his god. When all the tribes gathered, Sitting Bull purified himself through fasting and prayer. Then he took a sweat bath and wiped his body with sage. Next followed the pipe ceremony. He sat down and leaned against the sacred tree. Already weak from fasting, he was helped by his nephew, Jumping Bull. Holding still and showing no pain, Sitting Bull had Jumping Bull gouge his flesh to honor the Great Spirit. Starting on the bottom of his left arm, Jumping Bull used a bone awl; the point was driven into Sitting Bull's skin to rip out a chunk of flesh about the size of a nail head. Jumping Bull worked up and around the arm until over fifty pieces of flesh were taken. Then he started on the right arm in the same manner. Sitting Bull bled and his arms were wiped with sage. By the time the process was over, more than one hundred pieces of flesh had been removed.

Weak from fasting and loss of blood, Sitting Bull got up and danced about the sacred tree; the pain must have been acute. As tradition mandated, he stared into the sun for some time and then had another vision, which he related to his people. Again he saw dead soldiers and a victory by the people. He cautioned his people not to take any spoils. The blue coats would come into their valley, but they would come upside down. The troops would be killed, but some braves would be killed, too. He saw them upside down. It would be a victory for the people, but again, they must not plunder or mutilate the dead soldiers; this part was clear. If they did, sadness would befall them and sooner or later they would become more dependent upon the whites.

Coupled with the earlier vision, this was quite an omen, since his first vision came before the Indians knew the soldiers were in the field. Later, when the scouts brought back reports of General Crook's approach, the Sioux, confident of victory, prepared to defend themselves at the Rosebud.

Up to that point Sitting Bull's part in this drama had been invoking the god's will for his people—plus he foretold the threat. He had a vision, warned his people, and gave flesh. At forty-five, he was considered an old man and was not expected to be an active warrior. He had played his part as a holy man and a spiritual leader and was too important to lose in battle. His war record was so replete that he had nothing to prove. His arms were so swollen from the Sun Dance, he could hardly move them, let alone ride in battle against generals or draw a bow string. During the Battle of the Rosebud, he rode to the battle and encouraged his braves, but he didn't fight. A little more than a week later, when the Battle of the Little Bighorn occurred, his arms were recovering but hardly in fighting form. He was in the forefront from time to time, but his duty was to pray and encourage the braves. After all, the serious fighting was a young man's task and he was an old-man chief. It wasn't as if his people were without military guidance. His good friend and strongest ally, Crazy Horse, was a most capable war leader.

Sitting Bull might have shot at soldiers on an opposite hill or even finished off the odd wounded blue coat, but his most important job was to protect the women and children—and pray for success. When Reno attacked the village directly, Sitting Bull was likely still a formidable foe. When the battle was over, it was said that he was the one who told his people to let some of the soldiers get away. They had done enough. He no doubt warned his people, again, to avoid looting and mutilating, but in their victorious

Library of Congress, LC-USZ62-109538

Sitting Bull holding peace pipe

frenzy, they did not heed his words. And in the aftermath of the horrific battle, the American press created a picture of Sitting Bull as a villain on the Plains. After being hounded and starved, after taking his people to Canada for four years, hoping to find a home in the Grandmother's Land (his name for Queen Victoria), Sitting Bull, the last of the Sioux chiefs, surrendered his rifle in July 1881. He was held as a prisoner at Fort Randall for two years before he was allowed to return to Standing Rock. But he was never a broken man. Still the lance and shield to his people, he fought for them until he was murdered just before the massacre at Wounded Knee.

COMANCHE: THE MOST FAMOUS HORSE IN THE WEST

Did a horse named Comanche really survive the Battle of the Little Bighorn? What made this animal so legendary? Has Comanche been preserved for future generations?

Comanche wasn't an average cavalry-issue horse. Captain Myles Keogh's personal beast, he was a well-trained, splendid mount that stood out in a herd. Comanche was a bay, born sometime during the Civil War, probably around 1862. He was a little over fifteen hands high and weighed well over nine hundred pounds. Over the years he had collected an impressive number of battle scars from his adventures in the Indian wars, where he earned his name. Comanche was injured by an arrow during a skirmish with Indians in the Cimarron country near Bluff Creek (southeast of Dodge City, Kansas). He let out a bellow uncharacteristic for a hooved creature. His cry of pain sounded a lot like the scream of a charging Comanche warrior. Comanche was known for his stamina and courage, as well as his ability to get by on cheat grass or willow bark just like an Indian pony. He was readily identifiable and known to most of the men in the Seventh Cavalry.

Captain Myles Keogh was a man who loved good horses, and he took excellent care of his mount. He and Comanche were an inseparable pair on numerous adventures and campaigns into Indian country. Keogh was also one of the most interesting men in the famous Seventh Cavalry. He was born in Ireland in 1840, and like a good Irish boy of his age, he loved strong drink, a good fight, and the Catholic Church. He also hated England and bullies. After a few lackluster years in college, he longed to test his hand against the world, so he sailed for Africa and adventure. Later, when the pope called for good Catholics to defend the "Holy See" (the Papal states around the Vatican), young Myles took the first ship to Europe. He quickly rose to the office of lieutenant in the Papal Army. He fought valiantly and was awarded the *Medaglia di Pro Petri Sede* by the pope, himself, for bravery against the Piedmontesel, which he wore proudly.

By the time he received the cross from the pope, the American Civil War had started and that sounded exciting. He boarded a ship for the United States and promptly joined the Union Army. His Civil War record was distinguished. He quickly rose to the rank of major. After the surrender he was mustered out of the Union Army. At a loss as a civilian, he joined up again a year later as a captain to seek his fame and fortune on the Great Plains fighting the "hostiles." There he became associated with the flamboyant George Armstrong Custer, another former Civil War officer who was now seeking his fame on the Plains. The two men developed a mutual appreciation for each other—including a respect and love for fine horses.

Indeed it may have been Keogh who first sang "Garry Owen" to Custer, the song that became the anthem for the Seventh Cavalry. "Garry Owen" was a catchy, bawdy, drinking song with an Irish origin near Keogh's hometown. In Elizabeth Bacon Custer's memoirs, she suggests this happened when both men were stationed at Fort Riley, Kansas. She thought it was probably Myles Keogh's idea to start a regimental band. George Custer found it a splendid idea, since he liked music, and contributed the first fifty dollars for instruments. The Seventh Cavalry band became a permanent part of the regiment, accompanying the soldiers on numerous campaigns.

When on campaign in the West, Keogh and Comanche were always in the thick of battle. The captain was unquestionably a brave man, a characteristic that Custer appreciated. The Irishman drank heavily, but his drinking apparently didn't impair his duty. He also suffered from bouts of depression, but was, for the most part, a jovial companion.

Because of unrelated Indian accounts recorded at a later date, we have a good idea where the two famous soldiers made their stand at Little Bighorn. Custer, of course, had divided his command into three battalions. Captains Benteen and Reno crossed Ash Creek with their troops. The plan was to attack the Indians in a three-prong charge. Each battalion was quickly bogged down. Custer's command charged into the village and found stiff resistance. They were forced to retreat up the nearest hillside and make a stand. Legend may have overdramatized Keogh's sad end. One version says that the Irishman fought like a wildcat to the very end and was the last of his troops to die. An army scout who came upon the scene a few days later said it looked like he was indeed the last to fall. This same scout, at a later date, said he interviewed some Sioux braves who confirmed his statement. It's a good story and it may be true, but no one knows for sure. Further newspaper reports suggested that the fighting Irishman dropped a warrior with each load in his six-gun. One writer said, "A flame of coal blazed his eyes. His teeth glistened like a fighting grizzly bear." Never mind that the writer in question was two thousand miles away at the time of the battle.

One brave questioned a few years later says, conversely, that Keogh was one of the first of the group to go down, taking a couple of slugs from the opposing ridge. But perhaps the most believable account of Keogh's end was that told by a Sioux brave named Little Soldier, who was watching the troopers from another ridge. He said a slug hit Comanche, passed through the horse, and shattered Captain Keogh's knee. No longer able to stand, Keogh kneeled down, holding the reins of his well-trained mount, and returned fire from under his horse. He finally went down when several bullets fatally struck him, still holding desperately to the horse's reins.

Little Soldier came to take his horse since it looked like such a fine mount, but he didn't want to take an animal held by a dead man, which he considered bad medicine. Apparently others felt that way too. Comanche was not led away by any of the victorious warriors that afternoon. Keogh was, in fact, one of the few men in the Seventh whose fallen body wasn't mutilated. He was stripped of his clothes and boots, but the cross he wore may have saved his body from the fate that befell so many men on that hot June afternoon. The Sioux would have been familiar with such a cross and may have considered it strong medicine—a sign to leave Keogh's body alone. The battlefield wasn't a pretty sight. The frustration the Indians felt after years of broken treaties and the violation of their homeland, seethed over. The soldiers had attacked them. Nearly every man was scalped and brutally mutilated. Wounded men were tortured. Every piece of useful clothing or gear was stripped from the dead men. Custer had his ears pierced with awls so he could hear better in the next life (so he would learn to keep his word).

The stories and legends that surround the Battle of the Little Bighorn often give readers the impression that Comanche was the only Seventh Cavalry horse that survived the battle—but that's not true. The Sioux warrior, Gall, said the Sioux rounded up 100 to 150 cavalry horses that day. When the reinforcements finally arrived on the killing fields, they also collected a number of mounts that the braves had overlooked in their hasty retreat. They also disposed of the wounded animals that were suffering or could not join the march back to the fort. Most horses were shot if their injuries were at all debilitating.

Comanche was discovered in an arroyo, riddled with bullet and arrow wounds. Captain Keogh's saddle was upside down, hanging under the horse's belly, and the pad and saddle blanket were missing. Eastern reporters wrote that he was wounded seven times in all, which became an accepted fact—but we're really not sure. He was severely injured, and when the troopers found him, there was talk of shooting him to put him out of his misery. However, since he was such an excellent horse, an officer decided that the troopers should try to save him if they could. With some effort the soldiers were able to carefully get the wounded Comanche to a riverboat called the *Far West*, anchored at the mouth of the Little Big Horn River. Close to death, he was brought to Fort Abraham Lincoln (near Mandan, North Dakota), no longer able to walk by himself. With tender care and a sling to suspend him, it took nearly a year for the beast to fully recover. When he was in good shape, the officers decided that he had earned the right to be retired from active duty. He enjoyed being ridden by the children of the fort and became a four-legged celebrity.

In 1878, however, several children had an argument over who was to ride him, and the company commander decided that out of respect for his service, he should never be ridden again. "Comanche was," he said, "the only living representative of the bloody tragedy of Little Bighorn. His kind treatment and comfort should be a matter of pride and solicitude on the part of the Seventh Cavalry, to the end, that his life may be prolonged to the utmost limit . . . he will not be ridden by any person whatsoever under any circumstances." His words helped seal the legend of Comanche. A living mascot for the battle, for fifteen years Comanche walked in parades draped in black, black cavalry boots pointing backwards draped on the saddle, symbolizing the loss of Custer's Battalion.

So Comanche lived his last years in ease. He had the run of the fort and was allowed to eat out of the garbage barrels at will. When his caretaker and friend, Gustave Knave, was shot and killed at the Battle of Wounded Knee, the poor horse felt (or so the legend is told) the loss and his health started to deteriorate. Stable hands and hostlers believed the beloved old warhorse missed his friend. On November 7, 1891, Comanche passed on to that giant parade ground in the sky. He was nearly thirty years old.

Monuments to General Custer and his brave men who fell about him, Custer Battlefield, Montana

The Seventh wanted Comanche to be a permanent part of the regiment, so they looked for a way to preserve him. They contacted a Mr. Dyche from the University of Kansas, who consented to do the taxidermy job for four hundred dollars. Mr. Dyche, who was also a noted naturalist, came to the fort and took the horse's remains back to his studio. When the job was done, the taxidermist, proud of his job, told the army that if they wanted to donate the horse to the university, there would be no charge for his services. Funds were a little short, shipping costs were high, and the Seventh was due for a move. The soldiers reluctantly agreed to let Comanche stay in Kansas.

In 1893 a stuffed Comanche became a symbol of all that was true and brave. He was exhibited at the Chicago Expo for the world to see. Afterwards he returned to the museum of natural history at the University of Kansas, though interested parties have tried to

Comanche survived the Custer Massacre, 1876

John C. H. Grabill, photographer, Library of Congress (LC-USZ62-11937)

acquire him ever since. The Custer National Monument wanted the old warhorse for their museum, while the Seventh Cavalry wanted him placed at Fort Riley, Kansas. Interestingly enough, a Kiwanis Club in Montana also thought he'd be a noteworthy addition to their town. One can still visit Comanche at the University of Kansas. He's preserved behind climate-controlled glass.

While Comanche may not be the most famous horse in the Old West, he's certainly the most famous horse in the United States Cavalry. He's been the subject of numerous pieces of fiction and nonfiction, including a Walt Disney movie. In his day writers boasted that this noble steed was the only survivor from the Battle of the Little Bighorn (although quite a few Sioux would beg to differ). More correctly, Comanche was the most noted four-legged survivor from the doomed Custer Battalion.

JAMES BUTLER "WILD BILL" HICKOK: THE GUNMAN WHO HELD THE DEAD MAN'S HAND

Was Wild Bill Hickok the greatest gunfighter in the West? Did he kill a hundred men as he and his biographers have claimed? Did Hickok really fight off ten men at the Rock Creek Station in Nebraska?

During the hot summer of 1876, Wild Bill Hickok found himself in Deadwood, Dakota Territory, where he quickly set up shop in the Number 10 Saloon. Normally a cautious man, Bill took a seat with his back to the door—something he rarely did. With fifty dollars in chips borrowed from his friend the bartender, the ailing frontier legend soon had a poker game going with local gamblers. He was married now and was trying to gather a nest egg. He could still read the cards but his eyesight was getting dimmer. What he saw in front of him was his luck changing. He had a good hand.

It was then that Jack McCall, a man who carried a grudge, a man who wanted a reputation, came into the Number 10 and saw Wild Bill. It was a perfect opportunity. Without warning, he walked up to Wild Bill and shot him in the back of the head with his pistol. Not a good way for a famous gunman to go. Hickok fell dead, bleeding profusely. His cards fell to the floor—two black eights, two aces, one jack—now known as the famous "Dead Man's Hand."

Wild Bill Hickok was a living legend of the frontier. He was supposed to have killed scores and scores of bad guys in standup gunfights and untold numbers of Indians. Many people believed that the world was a better place because of the rugged gunfighter's aim. When asked about being a gunfighter, Hickok told a reporter that as far as killing went, he never thought about it because he didn't believe in ghosts. He said, "It's the other man or me."

On another occasion in Kansas, he told the famous journalist Henry Stanley, "No, by Heaven. I never killed one man without good cause. I would be willing to take my oath on the Bible tomorrow that I have killed over a hundred."

Henry Stanley, the reporter for the *Weekly Missouri Democrat* (who later went to Africa and uttered the immortal words, "Dr. Livingston, I presume?") was impressed by the dashing Hickok and did his share to expand Wild Bill's reputation as the gun-toting plainsman. Stanley's stories of Wild Bill's adventures, as narrated by Hickok himself, were wildly popular. The spirited scout could tell such a captivating, convincing tale that even the implausible seemed true. Few doubted the truth of the songs and stories that sprang up around the gunfighter.

There is no question that Wild Bill was a courageous man, a lawman who demonstrated his courage in a number of challenging situations. He was also a fine scout (for both the Union Army in the Civil War and the US Cavalry during the Plains Indian Wars). He was a crack shot and calm under fire. But like his good friend George Armstrong Custer, he had a gift for self-promotion and hyperbole.

Wild Bill was great copy.

Journalists flocked to him for a story and were rarely disappointed. He made a great first impression, and his quiet, charming style was ingratiating. So were his genteel manners—somewhat out of place in a gun-toting frontiersman. He wasn't a big mouth, or a braggart, in the usual sense . . . but he could spin a story. Bill was savvy enough to let the interviewer draw a story out of him, albeit embellished, so that it was believable. As a result, his reputation and his deeds snowballed in each retelling, and no one bothered to check the facts. Wild Bill became larger-than-life, and an interested public couldn't get enough of this man with the smoking Colts and the white hat who fought for truth and righteousness.

While Mr. Hickok was a willing participant in the creation of these frontier fairy tales, he wasn't the only culpable party. Journalists, eager to outdo their colleagues, felt free to add extravagantly to a tale to make their version more fantastic. Wild Bill surely had a hard time recognizing himself in print, but he owed his reputation to the press, and he knew it. He was never too busy to have a drink with a reporter.

Besides courting the press, Hickok also knew how to cultivate the good opinion of important people. He served with General George Armstrong Custer for nearly six months as a civilian scout in Kansas. Both men respected each other's ambition and shared a mutual admiration (also good copy). The general wrote the following about Hickok:

Of his courage there could be no question. His skill in the use of rifle and pistol was unerring. His deportment was exactly the opposite of what we expected for a man of his surrounding. It was entirely free of bluster and bravado. He seldom spoke of himself unless requested to do so. His influence among frontiersmen was unbound, his word was law. I have personal knowledge of at least half a dozen men whom he has at various times killed.

Mrs. Elizabeth Custer, also influenced by his physical charm and personable ways, also aware of the value of good copy, had this to say about the celebrated scout and gun fighter:

Physically he was a delight to look upon. Tall, lithe and free in every motion. . . . He was rather fantastically clad but that seemed perfectly in keeping with the time and place. He did not make an armory of his waist, but carried two pistols. He wore top-boots, riding breeches, and a dark blue flannel shirt, with a scarlet set in front.

Behind the wild stories that pervaded the popular press of the time was a true story worthy of telling. During the Civil War James Butler Hickok was a scout and a spy, and he served with distinction. He pulled off a number of daring jobs that got him the nickname Wild Bill—a name that stuck with him for the rest of his life. He lived up to his sobriquet while he was visiting a friend in Chicago in 1865. The two buddies were at a local watering hole shooting pool and drinking too much.

Bill was dressed in frontier attire: long hair, buckskin breeches, and moccasins. Some local toughs started to make fun of his appearance. He let the insults slide for a time, but the men wouldn't stop.

One of them asked, "Does everyone on the frontier pick his teeth with a Bowie knife?" Bill apparently replied, "No. But everyone knows who his father is!" The men moved in on Bill, who calmly turned his hickory pool cue around and proved how wild he could be.

In 1867 he was living in Springfield, Missouri, a rough town after the Civil War. The Union troops returning from the battlefield took it upon themselves to punish and avenge anyone even slightly connected with the Confederate raiders that had terrorized the state during the war (Quantrill's and Bloody Bill's groups). As a border state Missouri had been sharply divided between Unionists and Secessionists during the conflict, and moonlight hangings of gray sympathizers were common. One night over cards and whiskey in the old Lyon House, Bill had a serious conflict with a gambler named David Tutt. Their mutual interest in a woman named Susanna may have exacerbated the tension (Wild Bill had a reputation as a womanizer). Tutt was also a Southerner who had fought with the First Arkansas Infantry, while James Butler had been a Union man. The two men had met several years earlier, perhaps while Bill was working undercover in the South.

From this point on it is hard to separate fact from fiction.

Tutt supposedly had lost a fair amount of money in that evening's game, and he reminded Bill of an old forty-dollar debt, which Bill reportedly had repaid. A little later Tutt supposedly told Bill he still owed him thirty-five dollars from a horse sale. Bill countered and said it was only twenty-five. Angrily, Tutt took Bill's Waltham pocket watch as payment—apparently it was lying on the poker table. Harsh words were spoken and one formally challenged the other to a traditional fight of honor.

Near sundown the next evening, the two met in the dusty, crowded street. We know there was a gunfight, but the finer details were a bit blurred by black powder smoke. One man who observed the fight says they walked to a distance of seventy-five yards—which seems a long way for a pistol duel—to utter their last words. A man named Barnett wrote in his journal that they were maybe a hundred paces apart. George Nichols, whose stories would make Bill famous, says it was fifty feet.

What they said before the shooting is also open to debate. One observer has Hickok telling David Tutt to save his life, turn around, walk away . . . and live. Apparently David answered by pulling his revolver and firing, but not surprisingly at that range, his shot went wild. At this point, Bill drew and fired—some say with his left hand, others say he used his right. Some think he took a two-handed grip; others say Bill rested his heavy Colt on a handy fence. Barnett writes that both men fired at the same time. Regardless of the details, Tutt took a fatal slug in the chest and died on the spot. Bill got to tell the story his way.

Hickok was quickly cleared in the Tutt shooting and became something of a local celebrity. The Springfield duel, now more appropriately called a "standup" gunfight, was the true beginning of the Wild Bill Hickok legend because it got him noticed by journalists. After the shooting Hickok met the man who would change his life. His name was Colonel George Ward Nichols. The colonel supposedly watched the gunfight, and afterward, the two hit it off almost instantly. Over drinks, Bill told the Colonel about an incident that had taken place nearly five years earlier before he joined the Union Army at Rock Creek Station in Southeastern Nebraska. Nichols retold the story in an article for *Harper's,* and this version became the basis for the many Wild Bill Hickok stories that followed.

In Wild Bill's revisionist recounting of the story the events at Rock Creek Station became an epic struggle of good and evil, with Bill, of course, wearing the white hat. He found an eager audience in Nichols, a journalist who, like nearly all journalists past and present, was more interested in a good story than the absolute truth.

What really happened at Rock Creek was a far cry from Nichols's report in print. In 1861 Hickok was working for the Russell, Majors & Waddell Overland Stage Company in the Southwest. Somewhere along the line, if legend is correct, Hickok tangled with a silvertip grizzly. He supposedly fought the bear with a pistol and a Bowie knife. He killed the bear, but he was ripped up pretty badly in the process. The Overland Stage Company sent him to the Rock Creek Station in Southeastern Nebraska to convalesce and perform light duties. Because of the conflict between the North and South, and the expense of keeping open a large stage line, business wasn't as good as Russell, Majors & Waddell had hoped.

When Hickok arrived, Horace Wellman was managing the Rock Creek Station with the assistance of his wife and a hired man named "Doc" Brink. The Overland Stage Company owed money to a farmer named McCanles for land McCanles had sold them at Rock Creek, and their payment was overdue. The angry farmer accused Wellman of absconding with his money and promised to throw all those concerned with the company off the land if the debt wasn't settled by a given date.

Legend has it that McCanles didn't like Hickok. There is some suggestion that they were after the same woman. Perhaps they also had ideological differences over the impending war. Wild Bill was an affirmed Unionist—having helped, reportedly (think good copy), slaves escape on the Underground Railroad—while McCanles was an avowed Confederate.

On the summer day in question, McCanles came to collect his money, bringing his twelve-year-old son, a cousin named James Woods, and his hired farmhand, James Gordon. Wellman wasn't a brave man and there was no money in the coffers to pay off the farmer. He and his wife spinelessly decided to leave the job to the semi-recovered Hickok and timidly went out to work in the garden. McCanles was ready for a fight.

Things seemed to start well enough that hot summer day. When McCanles asked for some water, Bill got him a drink, though we don't know whether he invited the man into the station or brought a cup to him outside. McCanles was unarmed, since he liked to do his bullying with his mouth and back up his words with his fists. He may have teased Bill or threatened him; we don't know. He may have made a physical advance. Bill was still weak from his tangle with the grizzly and wasn't anxious to fight the large, muscle-bound sodbuster. Whatever occurred, Bill drew his pistol and shot the farmer in the chest—either from behind a curtain separating the rooms of the cabin or through the window curtain while the man stood outside.

McCanles's son ran to his father and held him while he died. As Woods ran to the dying man, Bill fired at him, too, but it wasn't a fatal shot. Woods went down, but then got up and ran for cover. Wellman and his wife, hearing the shots, returned from the garden. Mrs. Wellman shouted, "Kill him!" (referring to the escaping Woods). Woods was bleeding and not hard to follow. Station

Manager Wellman brutally beat the wounded Woods to death with his garden hoe, possibly partially severing his head from his body. Gordon tried to escape, too, but he was hunted down. He begged for his life but likely took both barrels from "Doc" Brink's shotgun while he was on his knees. The McCanles's son, David, was chased and beaten by Mrs. Wellman, who appears to have been a rather bloodthirsty sort, but he escaped into the thick woods.

Many feel that Hickok should have been tried for murder, or at the very least, manslaughter. He wasn't acting like a dime-novel hero in a white hat. The station keeper and his wife should not have abdicated their responsibility to a convalescing employee. Perhaps the killing of McCanles was self-defense. He was a known bully and he had made threats that might not have been idle. Nevertheless Hickok probably shot Woods, who was unarmed. If he did, this was uncalled for and cowardly, as was failing to prevent Wellman from beating the man. Or did Bill help "Doc" hunt down the frightened Gordon? Was he a party to the double-barrel killing? There is no way the last killings could be justified or condoned. A real hero would have stopped the slaughter.

Regardless of the truth, when Colonel Nichols wrote his piece for *Harper's*, he had the McCanles Gang (he spelled it M'Kandles) attack the station in force. Of course the mob of lawless men was well-armed. Bill and the bad guys fought hand-to-hand and with pistols, but in the end, Wild Bill saved the day and preserved the honor of the station against overwhelming odds, perhaps even saving Mrs. Wellman's virtue.

Later, J. W. Buel in the *Kansas City Journal* would build upon the story. He had Wild Bill kill ten outlaws. However this time the hero, himself, tragically took four bullets, suffered some knife wounds, and sustained a serious skull fracture. Later, in the *Saturday Evening Post*, among other magazines, Hickock's exploits were even more heroic. Dime novels also started to flood the market, "true life" stories of the great gunfighter-plainsman. In *Wild Bill, The Pistol Deadshot* by Prentiss Ingraham, the famous dime novelist had Bill shoot eleven bad guys at Rock Creek Station.

In 1867, with his reputation preceding him, Wild Bill headed to Kansas and became a US deputy marshal, working mostly out of Fort Riley. It was there that he met and became friends with General and Mrs. Custer. One of his duties was to track down and bring back army deserters. This was a serious problem not just for the Seventh Cavalry, but throughout the army; in some units as many as 10 to 25 percent of the troops might "skip," especially in the spring. While at Fort Riley he met and became good friends with Bill Cody—Buffalo Bill Cody— another man who would help change his life. Hickok hired Cody in March of 1868 to help him bring back a load of deserters. Not long after this, Wild Bill hired himself out to the Seventh as a civilian scout for one hundred dollars a month—a good wage in those days—to chase Indians.

By 1869 he became the sheriff of Ellis County, Kansas, the location of the wild cow town of Hays City. He carried his two Colts in his waistband, a conspicuous Bowie knife in his boot, and a short-barreled 12-bore shotgun. By now he'd given up his frontier duds and started to dress more like a drugstore dandy (he'd read too many of his own press clippings). He laid aside his buckskins and flannels and replaced them with black frock coats, fancy ruffled white shirts and ties, colorful, elegant vests, and tooled boots. He still wore his trademark hair long.

By 1871 Wild Bill was considered one of the "woolliest" men in the Wild West. He was hired to keep the peace in the untamed town of Abilene, Kansas, and he did. He made $150 a month, kept a percentage of the fines, and had an understanding that he could run his own gambling concerns on the side. His reputation kept things quiet. Thanks to the articles in *Harper's*, folks came to town just to shake his hand and make his acquaintance.

There is no question that Bill enjoyed the status he had achieved and played up the "wild" in the Wild Bill role. Hickok, like Custer, didn't seem to have the same "fear meter" most folks have. If he did feel this emotion, he never registered it. Nevertheless, he was a careful judge of character and seemed to know who he could push and who he could not. He never walked away from a fight, but he wasn't a fool, either. If a fight could be avoided, side-stepped, or if the numbers didn't add up, Bill looked for alternatives like busting a pool cue over his opponent's head.

A good example of this cool-headed nature was his first meeting with the young killer John Wesley Hardin who had come up from Texas with a herd. Before dying, the mercurial Hardin would reportedly kill forty men with his Colts (which is a gross exaggeration). The young lad came into Abilene looking like a poor cowhand with a broken-down hat, faded jeans, and down-at-the-heel boots. He was also wearing a brace of well-oiled guns in town, which was strictly against the law. When the over-dressed Hickok met Hardin, he saw something in the cowboy that set off an internal alarm. Perhaps there was a coldness in the Texan, or maybe

Hardin's budding reputation had preceded him. Certainly the killer cowboy knew of Hickok. Neither man was apparently intimidated by the other. Instead, it seemed there was a mutual affinity for the other as a fellow badass that led to an awkward friendship.

Wild Bill politely told Hardin he'd need to turn in his guns, something the trail-tired cowboy would not want to do. He was told he could have his Colts back when he left town. Onlookers say the situation got a little tense. Some accounts say that Hickok had his guns out, covering Hardin, when he made his request. However this doesn't make sense because Hickok couldn't take Hardin's weapons if his own hands were full of iron. Hardin, in his memoirs (which can't be trusted), says he handed over his guns butt-first when the lawman reached for them. Then the kid, who was supposed to be very fast, twirled them in his hands and drew both hammers back, covering the lawman with the big bores. Quick-thinking Bill told the young man that he was planning on buying the cowhand a few drinks. They went to the bar and bent elbows, becoming good friends. Hardin writes that Hickok told him, "[You] was the gamest and quickest boy I ever saw. Let's compromise this matter and I will be your friend. Let's go in here and take a drink, and I want to talk to you and give you some advice." A mutual respect developed between the two. It's a good story.

After accidentally killing his deputy during a shoot-out in a saloon, Wild Bill naturally lost interest in Abilene. This was one shooting Hickok assuredly felt sorry about. His deputy had a family, and they were good friends. He paid for the man's funeral. As far as we know, this was the last time James Butler Hickok ever drew his gun on another human being. He drifted and gambled. He took rich men and European royalty on elaborate buffalo hunts. He even agreed to put on some canned "buffalo hunts" for audiences in the East. These extravaganzas were forerunners of the Wild West shows that would soon be the rage.

In 1872 his good friend Buffalo Bill Cody asked him to join his theatrical production, *Scouts of the Plains.* The pay was good, but for a man who cut his teeth on a Bowie knife, sagebrush, and the smell of gun smoke, the "boards" and footlights were irritating. He especially hated the phony lines he was required to say. One night he stopped the show as he took a drink from a jug. He shouted out, "This is cold tea . . . I asked for whiskey!" These words weren't in the script, but the audience howled with delight. Bored, he started ad-libbing lines, which also elated the audience. He couldn't take New York much longer, so when his contract ran out he headed west.

As he traveled from town to town, he was still news, but by that time his eyes were starting to bother him. He wondered if the flashes and bright lights of the stage had damaged his sight. Poor vision was a problem for a man who had a reputation as a gunslinger. He would be an easy target for any tinhorn wanting to make a reputation. He saw several doctors who diagnosed his malady as a progressive form of glaucoma, most likely resulting from gonorrhea (Bill spent a lot of time with ladies of questionable virtue). The doctors told him his condition would get worse until he went blind.

That day as he sat in the Number 10 with his back to the door, the legend ended as another man attempted to take his place in Western myth. McCall was quickly tried in a miner's court and surprisingly acquitted. He drifted about, bragging about what he'd done, but he was arrested again in October and indicted for Hickok's murder. Wild Bill was a popular man and his friends were not happy with the previous trial. The prosecution said McCall couldn't claim double-jeopardy since he was tried on Indian land and in a miner's court. After an appeal to the territory supreme court, which was denied, McCall was hanged in January. Wild Bill was buried in Deadwood.

As Hickok once said in an interview, "Whenever you get into a row be sure and not shoot too quick. Take your time. I've known many a feller slip up for shootin' in a hurry." It's hard to be unruffled when bullets are whizzing about your head. Nevertheless, all mythology aside, Bill was fast and accurate. He could pull his pistols quickly—and more important, he could shoot with a rare degree of accuracy even when being shot at. But the metaphoric notches on his Colts were considerably fewer than his reading public dared suspect. The hundreds of men that he was supposed to have killed were an invention of the press. More realistically, we might have records of Bill being in six to seven standup gunfights. His body count might be eight men that we know of—it could even be six or seven, and a few of the fellows he killed were shot by accident.

While there's a lot of hype about the venerable Mr. Hickok, there are two consistent facts that arise from all the exaggeration. Bill was very cool under fire, and he was a damned deadly shot with either hand. Even after the bombast is swept away, Wild Bill is still one of our great Western legends.

Wild Bill Hickok

CALAMITY JANE: FACTS AND FICTIONS ABOUT MARTHA JANE CANARY

Was Calamity Jane married to Wild Bill Hickok as she claimed? Did she ride with the United States Cavalry as a muleskinner and a scout? Was she a teamster, a tramp, a fast gun, a drunk—or a misguided lady looking for a secure home?

Martha Jane Canary, aka Calamity Jane, bounced around the West as wild and woolly as any of her male contemporaries in the 1870s and 1880s. She worked odd jobs, often as a teamster—and apparently could curse as proficiently as any man in the profession. Around 1875 she passed herself off as a male to go on a geological expedition into the Black Hills with Professor Walter Jenny. The next spring she signed up as a muleskinner—still purporting to be a man—to go with General Crook into Montana after the Sioux.

Part of Calamity Jane's legend was that, like most of her male contemporaries, she didn't bathe too often, and you knew she was coming if you were downwind. On the Crook campaign, Jane was getting more than a little ripe, so she joined the men as they were having a bath. When it was soon discovered she was a woman, she was summarily sent home. The army didn't want females fraternizing with the troops, even if the female in question was a good teamster.

Like Wild Bill, Buffalo Bill Cody, or Billy the Kid, Calamity Jane was launched into the national eye by dime novels and stories in the tabloids—tales that played loosely with the truth. Fact and folklore are so intermingled in her story that they have to be carefully separated if one wants an accurate look at this icon of the West. Jane was known to mix up her stories, especially if she'd been nipping at her "snake bite" medicine.

In her autobiography, which is at best revisionist history mingled with fiction, she writes:

> I was born in Princeton, Missouri, May 1, 1852. Father and mother were natives of Ohio. I had two brothers and three sisters, I being the oldest of the children. As a child I had a fondness for adventure and outdoor exercise and especial fondness for horses which I began to ride at an early age and continued to do so until I became an expert rider.

We have to give her the benefit of the doubt on her birthday; however, there is some evidence to suggest that she may have been born in 1844. That she was a tomboy there can be little doubt. She enjoyed hunting, guns, horses, and the outdoors. She had little affinity for girlish clothes, dolls, or playing house.

Around 1865 her family left Missouri for greener pastures out west, heading for Virginia City, Montana. For the young Jane, the overland trip was a wonderful adventure. But it wasn't always pleasant. Her father was a heavy drinker who may have been abusive, so the young girl had to grow up fast. She assumed many of the domestic chores, and she also kept the family fed by shooting game. Her time on the trail helped hone her marksmanship and skill with livestock; it was also her first introduction to being a teamster. When her mother died near Blackfoot, Montana, the family headed for Salt Lake City.

There is a bit of speculation as to how Jane got her famous nickname. Some suggest it went back to her days in Salt Lake City. Shortly after their arrival, her father died, leaving her an orphan. One version of the legend says that folks called her "Calamity" Jane because of all the troubles that had befallen her. In her autobiography, though, she says she earned the name in 1872 while "in the army." She wrote:

It was during this campaign that I was christened Calamity Jane. It was on Goose Creek, Wyoming, where the town of Sheridan is located. Captain was in command of the post. We were ordered out to quell an uprising of the Indians and were out for several days, had numerous skirmishes during which six of the soldiers were killed and several severely wounded. Captain Eagan was shot. I was riding in advance and of hearing the firing, saw the Captain reeling in his saddle as though about to fall. I turned my horse and galloped back with all haste. I lifted him onto his horse in front of me and succeeded in getting him safely to the fort. Eagan recovering, laughingly said, "I name you Calamity Jane, the hero of the plains."

However she got her handle, it was a name she was proud of. It had a good ring with the Eastern press, too, and helped to build up a myth around her.

In her autobiography, Calamity Jane claimed she was in the army as early as 1870, serving as a scout with Custer, where she "donned the uniform of soldier." She said, "It was a bit awkward at first but I soon got to be perfectly at home in men's clothes." Whether she saved a seriously wounded Captain Eagan or went on dangerous missions is up for debate. Some suggest that it was whiskey talk, boasting, and yarning. Later she suggested that she went to the Southwest during the Indian campaigns there. She claimed to have been a daring scout, going on many dangerous missions, scouting, and riding express. Jane may well have been in the Southwest during these turbulent years, but it's hard to pin her down. On one occasion she says she met Custer in this region, which would have been quite a feat since he was never in the vicinity.

By the time of her mythical bath with the troops, our jaded heroine was no longer the skinny girl she had been in her teens— she had filled out a bit. And while she was never a raving beauty, even in men's clothing, she looked decidedly female. Did the men in the army need spectacles, or were they so focused on killing Indians they weren't looking straight? Was she so ugly that even hard-up soldiers wouldn't give her a glance? Maybe the officers really didn't know they had a woman in tow, but the enlisted did and supposedly kept it mum. Did a straight-laced officer walk by while Jane was cavorting with the men in the water and discover to his shock the muleskinner was a woman? Perhaps she was running a "business" on the side and the men had tired of her charms and this was a polite, official way of dismissing her.

It might have been good fortune that she was asked to leave. The Sioux had never been so restless. General Crook would soon face a strategic defeat at the hands of the Sioux and Cheyenne. A few days later General Custer would meet his doom in a place called the Little Big Horn. Apparently disgruntled by the ignominy of her untimely dismissal, Calamity Jane needed cheering up so she headed to the hottest boomtown in that part of the world, Deadwood, South Dakota.

While she was in Deadwood, she said she worked as a teamster transporting machinery and supplies to miners in the camps. She also carried the United States mail between Deadwood and Custer, a dangerous job because of the Indian situation. Her route was a fifty-mile run, one way, over a very rough trail through the Black Hills. She made her runs without complaint and in good time.

She said she met the dashing Wild Bill Hickok, a fixture at local gambling establishments. Jane claimed that Wild Bill was the love of her life, and that they married and had a child together, but this has never been verified. This was as likely as winning the lottery, but it made a really fine story for pulp writers. Bill was a ladies' man, but his ladies often had meters running. If there were any connubial delight between them, it would have been a random encounter. At one time Bill had been a plainsman, but he'd become a bit of a dandy as his reputation burgeoned. He liked fine apparel, something Calamity Jane didn't appreciate, and he bathed on a regular basis if possible. Bill liked his women frilly, feminine—and sweet smelling. In Deadwood, he and Calamity Jane *may* have talked, drunk some whiskey, and even played cards. It's doubtful that they "played house."

Of course, once Bill was dead, Calamity could say what she pleased about their relationship—no one was the wiser. This was a good public relations move on her part. The two legends together made great copy when united. Dime novelists got into the act and created stories that even Bill and Jane wouldn't recognize. For the rest of her life, Jane insisted that the fallen Hickok was her great love. In her "official" autobiography she tells us that she chased Bill's killer, Jack McCall, down the street and would have shot him if she hadn't left her Colts on her bedpost. She claims to have had the back-shooting McCall trapped in a butcher shop when the townspeople took him off to jail before she could rip him apart with her bare hands.

What we do know about Jane is she was kind, and willing to give a down-and-out family her last dollar. The townspeople in Deadwood remembered her actions during a serious smallpox epidemic. Calamity risked her own life, tirelessly nursing the afflicted back to health, asking for nothing in return. Doc Babcock said she was some sort of an angel—especially when dealing with sick children. "Oh, she'd swear to beat hell at them, but it was a tender kind of cussing."

There was no question that Martha Jane was an obnoxious drunk who liked to do wild things. But the stories, even by Calamity Jane standards, are a bit extreme. Once when drunk, she reportedly rode a bull down the main street of Rapid City. On another occasion, according to Charles E. Chaplin, Calamity and Arkansas Tom went to the opera house to see a play. When they got a little bored with the production, Calamity rolled some chewing tobacco in her mouth, working up a generous amount of spit. Moving closer to the stage, Jane hocked a big stream of brown tobacco juice at the actress's face, hitting her in the eye and dripping down her frilly dress—ruining it. The audience roared with delight. As a finale,

Arkansas Tom and Calamity Jane shot out a few of the lamps. According to legend, Jane and Tom walked out of the theater arm in arm, to the thundering applause of the audience.

Easterners were fascinated by the Wild West, especially the West they'd read about in dime novels. Capitalizing upon this romance was Buffalo Bill Cody and his Wild West Show. Cody hired Calamity Jane because he felt she could draw a crowd, thanks to the outlandish tales written about her. He regretted having to fire her because she couldn't hold her liquor. Jane had a predisposition for bravado and obnoxiousness; however, on stage her performance was overacted and rude. Even by Wild West show standards, she wasn't much of a performer. She was certainly nowhere near the caliber of showman as Cody or Hickok. Both Hickok and Buffalo Bill knew how to play their audiences and spun their romantic tales with skill and bravado. They also knew how to hold their liquor and keep their stories comparatively straight, something Jane couldn't do. While touring with the Palace Museum Show, Jane told a wonderful story about how she had saved Wild Bill Hickok, her supposed husband, from a plethora of gun-slinging bad guys. Of course, not a word of it was true. After one drunken appearance too often, she was fired.

As she got older, she fell deeper and deeper into the depths of alcoholism. With the help of a ghostwriter, she wrote her autobiography. She aligns herself with Custer and his campaigns—and of course, with Wild Bill. The book is mostly a lively work of fiction, the story of how she wished her life had been. In 1885 she married a stage driver named Clinton Burke, and the two had a daughter who was raised in a convent. In 1901 she portrayed "The Famous Woman Scout" at the Pan American Exposition in New York, but she got drunk and accosted some of the local policemen and was let go. In Montana she shot up a few bars and was asked to never come back.

All mythic hyperbole aside, Calamity Jane was a strong, flamboyant personality, with enough nerve to make her mark in a man's world. She could be kind and generous to a fault, but she was also bold, loud-mouthed, and vulgar. She had an obvious contempt for gender roles and social convention. She was a hard-drinking, tobacco-chewing, cigar-smoking, pistol-packing, buckskin-pants-wearing woman. Sometimes she worked as a bawd, broke horses, drove wagons, or rode dispatch. She was an excellent rider and a good shot. She enjoyed smoke-filled bars, cursed like a trooper, and was a very poor gambler.

Cheap whiskey and a hard life had taken a desperate toll on this desperate legend. It had not escaped her, in sober moments of reflective tranquility, that her life was not a storybook tale. So many had made money on her fictional yarning, and she often lived in abject poverty. Sometimes she slept in alleys and barns. Too often she didn't know where her next meal would come from. When she had had money, and she did on several occasions, she had foolishly squandered it on a drunk, buying drinks for the house, or on crooked games of chance. Too often this lonely, famous woman of the mythic West had resorted to prostitution in the lowest of whorehouses, the so-called "hog ranches" that catered mainly to frontier soldiers (even cowboys avoided such establishments).

Martha Jane also resorted to petty theft to survive. On more than one occasion she was arrested for shoplifting and thrown into jail. By the turn of the century, life had beaten her down. Sometimes

Martha Canary (Calamity Jane)

she was helped by friends—including a famous madam in the Dakotas. Secretly, all she had wanted was a good relationship with a man and a family of her own—she simply didn't know how to make it work. Friends say that she aged into an old woman almost overnight. She once said she wanted everyone to "leave me alone and let me go to hell my own route."

On August 1, 1903, the drunken cowgirl died dead broke. Deadwood, South Dakota, a town that had been good to her, honored her last wish, to be buried next to Wild Bill Hickok.

BILLY THE KID: VICIOUS KILLER OR VICTIM OF BAD PRESS?

Was Billy the Kid a cold-blooded murderer? Did he kill for the first time at twelve when a man insulted his prostitute mother? Did Billy have twenty-one bloody notches on his six-gun to match each year of his life?

Poor Billy the Kid was hardly cold in his grave when the first wave of books and articles about his legendary career flooded the market. Each story seemed to take a little more liberty with the truth than the last—and the readership ate his stories up. Not enough could be written about Billy, the Boy Bandit. An author didn't need to do much research—simply take the story the last fellow wrote and expand upon it in whatever ways one's imagination dictated. The stories got more and more outlandish.

Some of these legends are so rooted in the written word they die quite hard. One historic novelist said Billy was an Apache who was shot by Buffalo Bill with Wild Bill Hickok's famous Navy Colt. Within a month of his death, another novelist whose last name, coincidentally, was Fable, published a hastily constructed piece with the subtitle *The History of an Outlaw Who Killed a Man For Every Year of His Life*. Perhaps Fable heard that the Kid had killed twenty-one men, or, more likely, he simply made it up because it sounded good. He was probably the one who popularized the number and it stuck in the folklore.

The *Police Gazette*, a popular adventure story magazine, got into the act. So did Billy's nemesis, Pat Garrett, who had the help of a ghostwriter in crafting his gory story. He had killed Billy, after all, and because he was *there*, his account seemed accurate. His work has been the basis for a plethora of other texts—and myth has become inextricably linked with history ever since.

Folklore paints a portrait of young Billy as a good-looking pathological killer, the scourge of the New Mexico Territory. In spite of the myriad works of fiction and nonfiction written about the last years of his life, his early days are not well documented. Most evidence indicates that he was born in New York City in November of 1859. He was named Henry McCarty, the first son of Michael (some say Patrick) and Catherine McCarty. His parents apparently had come from Ireland during the potato famine and lived in the Irish slums of Manhattan.

Maybe it went like this: When Billy was a little boy, his father died, and pretty Catherine, Henry, and his younger brother, Joseph, moved to Indianapolis at the end of the Civil War. There she met Henry Antrim, a pleasant man, an express company driver, some years her junior. Not much is known about the romantic nature of their relationship, but it took a while to bud (at least on Catherine's part) and Henry was a patient suitor.

Catherine had a flair for business, was by all accounts a good mother, and provided a secure, loving home for her two boys. Billy didn't grow up in poverty, as some have written—suggesting he "was driven to a sordid life of crime." Nor was Catherine a prostitute, as some writers have noted. At different times Mrs. McCarty owned and operated boarding houses, hotels, laundries, and other service businesses; she made a good living from them. We know she moved from Indiana to Kansas, possibly even to New Orleans and Denver.

When Billy was twelve, while they were in Wichita, Kansas, Catherine was diagnosed with tuberculosis. In those days there was little hope for those afflicted with this disease. She sold off all her holdings and moved to Silver City, New Mexico, where it was said the dry climate of the high desert might help clear her lungs. Henry Antrim followed her and the family each time she moved, and it was here that she finally married, becoming Mrs. Henry Antrim. Antrim went to work in the mines while Catherine ran a boarding house until she became too sick to work.

While she was alive Catherine saw to it that her boys were well educated. Tony Connor, one of Billy's close friends said, "Billy got to be a reader. He would scarcely have his dishes washed until he would be sprawled out somewhere reading a book. It was the same down at the butcher shop [where he also worked]." He read the classics at the urging of his mother, but when she died he soon found adventure fiction more exciting. He devoured dime novels and the *Police Gazette*. Catherine had also made sure her boys knew how to write. Once he became notorious as an outlaw, he penned a number of letters to political officials defending his actions—and wrote defensive pieces for the papers. Consider a letter he wrote to Governor Wallace on December 12, 1880, not long before his death:

> I noticed in the *Las Vegas Gazette* a piece which stated that Billy "The Kid," the name by which I am known in this country, as the Captain of a band of outlaws who held forth

the Portales. There is no such Organization in Existence. So the Gentlemen must have drawn very heavily on their imagination. My business at White Oaks the time I was waylaid and my horse shot, was to see Judge Leonard who has my case in hand.

Billy was understandably upset by his mother's illness. He was lost when she died. During the last few months of her life, he suggested he was by her side, holding her during violent fits of coughing. Mrs. Truesdell, a family friend who helped care for Catherine McCarty, looked after the boys after their mother's death and gave Billy work at her hotel.

Billy was a good worker, and years later Mrs. Truesdell said that Billy was the only boy who never stole from her. But Billy craved adventure, and life working in the hotel soon bored him. Both Billy and Joseph liked their stepfather and called him Uncle Henry, but didn't look to him for direction. He was more like a loveable big brother than an authority figure. Mrs. Truesdell, with her own family and the hotel, probably wasn't sure what to do with the two boys. Bill went out on his own and drifted rather aimlessly from one place to another. He never really grew up—or had time to.

He eventually fell into petty crime. On one occasion, Billy and a friend broke into Charley Sun and Sam Chung's laundry and stole a bundle of clothes. Billy was caught red-handed and turned over to the sheriff. The sheriff, thinking he would "scare Billy straight," was pretty tough on him. Billy panicked, climbed up a chimney, and escaped. Had Uncle Henry Antrim, or even Mrs. Truesdell, taken control of the situation and disciplined the young thief at this point, we might never have heard of Billy the Kid.

But in spite of his early turn toward crime, Billy was not the vicious killer made out in legend and song—nor was he a poster boy for the Boy Scouts. He might have killed four men, but those were shootings he would have considered self-defense or justified. He wasn't mentally deranged, as so many of his biographers have suggested. Western heroes, Bat Masterson, Wyatt Earp, and Wild Bill Hickok, for example, were more deserving of a bloody reputation, but Billy the Kid made one large, costly mistake as a teenager. He picked the wrong side in the Lincoln County War.

Billy wasn't a saint by any stretch of the imagination. He stepped outside the law. Sometimes he did and said foolish things, acting tough without thinking about the consequences. And he rode with some unsavory characters. But he wasn't a homicidal maniac; rather, he was carefree and irresponsible and he made some stupid choices. He was reportedly the sort who would gladly help you out of a snow bank, give a down-and-out drifter a dollar—or take a few cattle if he needed eating money. He was a fun-loving young man who loved music and dances and the affections of the young ladies. He also had some leadership qualities. But he would become famous because he was one of the political pawns in a brutal range war so bloody it caught the attention of the national press and the interest of the American public—and his side lost.

Not much is known about Billy's movements around 1875. We think he drifted, wandering about the Southwest. He presumably gambled, did odd jobs, and worked as a ranch hand, learning the cowboy trade. He surely rustled an occasional steer or horse when the opportunity arrived. The drifter surfaced in Arizona near Camp Grant on November of 1876. There he worked on the

Hooker ranch and then at the Miles Wood Hotel. In Globe City he "found" a horse (undoubtedly it had "wandered off" after he untied it) that was the property of a tough army sergeant who didn't take kindly to horse thieves. The cavalryman filed a complaint with the justice of the peace. A warrant was issued and Billy found himself behind bars. Again, rather than face up to his sins, his first thought was flight. He threw a handful of salt in the guard's eyes and ran like a scared rabbit. He was quickly recaptured. To make sure he'd be around to stand trial, the sheriff took the young thief to the local blacksmith and had him shackled. That night, when the guard checked on the prisoner, he was gone, shackles and all.

But petty crime soon gave way to more serious behavior. The Kid drifted into Arizona, patronizing the George Atkins Saloon. One of the regulars was a blacksmith who worked at Camp Grant, a bully named Francis "Windy" P. Cahill. One day in the late summer, Windy came in and started to rough up the Kid's hair, something he'd done before. But today he didn't stop at that. He started to get abusive. He slapped the boy then threw him to the ground and dove on top of him, pinning the lad. To a boy raised on pulp fiction and romanticism, such actions were a serious insult and required a response in kind, but the man weighed twice as much as Billy—and was strong. They rolled around the floor until Billy was able to get an arm loose and free his revolver, a .45 Colt. Jamming the barrel into the blacksmith's side, he pulled the trigger. The report of the firearm was deafening in the saloon. Windy let go and Billy slipped out. He had killed his first man.

Again, panicking, Billy ran from the saloon and rode out of town as fast as he could, instead of staying to straighten things out. There might have been a territorial grand jury, but in that day, what he'd done would have been considered an honest shooting, a clear case of self-defense. Few juries in the West would have convicted him. However, because he ran and didn't stay around for the inquest, he was wanted for questioning. To escape his troubles, Billy left Arizona and rode east into history and legend. He also changed his name. He'd been going by the nickname Kid, Kid Antrim, or later The Kid. Kid, of course, was a handle that stuck with him. But he now took up another famous alias, William (Billy) Bonney.

He found himself in Southeastern New Mexico, specifically, Lincoln County, a wild tract of land bigger than South Carolina with fewer than two thousand inhabitants. This was a land without law, where only the fittest survived, taking what they could by force. Empires were being carved out and held by Samuel Colt's great equalizer. In Lincoln County, Billy went to work at the Tunstall Ranch. He idolized the British rancher, John Tunstall, a man who was trying to make his mark in the harsh new territory. Billy looked up to the man as the father he never had. He worked hard and was considered a top hand.

The Lincoln County War was a watershed for Billy. It started in 1878, but its roots went back much further. In the 1870s L. G. Murphy and James Dolan started to monopolize the local economy. They controlled the bank and the store, and held lucrative beef contracts with Fort Stanton. They were supported by several important "silent partners" in high places, including US Attorney

Thomas Catron and Lincoln County Sheriff William Brady. Also on their payroll were a number of outlaws, including the savage Jess Evans and his Seven Riders Gang. This consortium of businessmen and cutthroats liked to call themselves the "House."

The House was opposed by another group of businessmen headed by cattle baron John Chisum, attorney Alexander McSween, and rancher/entrepreneur John Tunstall. This group called themselves the "Regulators." They countered the House by starting their own general store and bank. The new bank and store did quite well, which naturally angered the House. Murphy and Dolan felt they had to take action. They ordered Sheriff Brady to arrest Tunstall on a phony charge of horse stealing. After the Englishman was disarmed, anxious members of the Sheriff's posse, most likely Jess Evans or his gang, shot down the unarmed man. A blood bath ensued.

Billy was nineteen years old when John Tunstall was brutally murdered. "They killed Mr. Tunstall," he said to a friend. "They shot him down like a dog. He's in the Sanchez Canyon." His friends noticed that when Billy reported the incident, he was so nervous and upset he could not sit down. He vowed to get those responsible for the crime.

He held Sheriff Brady personally accountable since the killers were under his direction, but he wasn't ready to take the law into his own hands. The intensity of the infamous Lincoln County War heightened. The region divided into armed camps. The Lincoln County justice of the peace, John Wilson, had issued warrants for the arrest of Jess Evans and other members of his gang. Sheriff Brady ignored the orders, so Justice Wilson gave the warrants to the

Lincoln County constable, Antonio Martinez, who asked Billy to help him serve the legal documents.

Billy thought himself a soldier in a cause he felt was just; he was more determined than ever to right the wrongs that had been committed. In his mind he was a romantic warrior in an epic struggle between good and evil. He was incensed by the hypocrisy and corruption that he had witnessed, and he was rapidly losing faith in the system of justice—a system whose loyalties went to the highest bidder in the wide-open county. Justice was something that he would administer with a Colt pistol and a Winchester rifle.

Sheriff Brady, of course, didn't honor Billy's deputy commission and threw him in jail. This didn't sit well with Billy who was, after a fashion, trying to do things in a quasi-legal manner. Martinez, Billy, and Fred Waite had ridden to James Dolan's ranch to arrest Jess Evans. Sheriff Brady was also there and managed to get the drop on Billy. He subsequently arrested Billy, Martinez, and Waite for disturbing the peace. Then he let Martinez go after disarming him. Billy and Fred were jailed. With nothing to hold him on, Brady finally let Billy out in a few days, but he kept Billy's beloved Winchester, something else Billy would not forget. Worse still, Billy couldn't attend Tunstall's funeral.

According to the Regulators, Sheriff Brady was guilty of Tunstall's murder, but a corrupt territorial governor and the big business interests that had invested heavily in the area protected him. On the morning of the first of April, six of the Regulators, including Billy Bonney, positioned themselves by a corral to wait for Brady and his deputy, George Hindman. When they approached, at around 9:00 a.m., Billy and his friends stood up and opened fire. Both lawmen were shot to death. Billy sustained a wound in the thigh.

Public opinion, which had been running in the Regulators' favor, started to turn the other direction, however. Ambushing the sheriff in the middle of town, even a corrupt sheriff, was a serious offense. Though the Regulators felt they had administered justice, in the eyes of the community, they had gone too far. As their informal leader, Billy got the credit for the murder. He had fired at Brady, but we are quite certain he didn't shoot the deputy—several of his associates who hated Hindman took credit for that. Billy's focus was on the man who orchestrated his boss's murder. There was now a price on his head.

When a new territorial governor was appointed, a federal investigator was appointed also. Billy was asked to turn state's evidence, which he gladly did after spending some time dodging deputies and bounty hunters. Billy allowed himself to be "taken," and he gave testimony about the Lincoln County War.

Although he was supposed to be given immunity, he instead became a political pawn. The Brady shooting kept coming up and wouldn't go away. It would be difficult for a savvy official to write it off in the face of public opinion and a vitriolic press. After a while, it looked as though Billy would never get himself cleared of the charges. Had he fled to Montana or Iowa, someplace far from Lincoln County, he could have drifted into obscurity. But he didn't. He stayed in his beloved Southwest.

By this time, Billy came to represent all that was wrong in Lincoln County, though he surely wondered why all the blatant murders committed by the other side had never been brought up. Finally, a politically ambitious Pat Garrett, who had just been elected sheriff by a narrow margin, vowed to bring him in. Mostly because of the press coverage surrounding the shootings, many folks felt that if Billy Bonney was behind bars and summarily hanged, order would be restored in this lawless land.

Billy wrote to newspapers and politicians arguing his case. It soon became obvious that everyone wanted him behind bars and then attached to a stout piece of hemp for the Brady incident. In December of 1880 Billy even argued his case before the governor, calling on him to keep his earlier promise and clear him of the charges. By then Governor Lew Wallace had written off the young outlaw in the name of political expediency. At that point, helping Billy would have been political suicide. He authorized a five-hundred-dollar reward for whoever brought him in.

Almost overnight the Kid's name became a national household word. W. S. Koogler of the *Las Vegas Gazette*, who shuddered over the anarchy in the region, felt like Billy was the focal point for lawlessness, and it was his duty as a God-fearing journalist to point it out—whether or not he had all the facts. It was Koogler who called him "Billy the Kid" in his scathing article, and the name stuck. His stories were picked up by larger papers, and before long, the handle was firmly entrenched in Western history.

When Garrett finally caught up with Billy, the young man knew that if he were going to keep breathing, he would have to break out of jail. Garrett had Billy put in a room next to his office with an armed guard. The two men who were assigned to watch the slippery lad were Bob Olinger and James Bell. Billy was taken to the blacksmith's and had his arms and legs shackled. "The Lincoln jail would hardly hold a cripple," Sheriff Garrett had said to his friends.

Garrett had warned the two jailers about Billy's slippery ways, but they didn't take him seriously. As Olinger said, "Billy has no more chance of escaping than he does of going to heaven." They apparently didn't know the Kid's hands were smaller than his wrists.

On April 28 while Olinger was at dinner, Billy asked Bell to take him to the privy. When they were out of sight, Billy slipped the cuff off one wrist and swung the chain and the other empty cuff as hard as he could at Bell's head. The man went down, but he wasn't out. The two fought for Bell's belly gun. Billy claimed he didn't want to hurt the jailer, but the man kept coming at him, and the gun went off, as guns in struggles tend to do. We're not sure if the shot was by accident or if Billy shot and killed Bell so he could escape. He went to the office to get the key to unlock his leg irons. After he freed himself, he grabbed Olinger's shotgun, which must have been in the corner. When Olinger returned, Billy shot him with both barrels and made his escape.

The Kid had killed two more men, arguably in self-defense since he felt he shouldn't have been jailed and was scheduled to hang. We really don't know. His escape was an embarrassment for the sheriff, who vowed to hunt Billy down again. In July Garrett finally caught Billy coming into a friend's house. In the dark room, he shot down the young outlaw. Billy the Kid was killed, but his legend has never died.

So much has been written on this boy bandit, it's hard to sift through the myth. By the time he was laid to rest, the amount of "yellow copy" about the young outlaw had hit tidal wave proportions. The truth about this lad is less sensational than folklore would have us believe. He didn't have twenty-one deadly notches to his credit; he didn't wear flashy outfits. He was always well groomed, weighed in at 135 to 140 pounds, was quite intelligent, quick witted, and clever. He was cheerful, but he

COURTESY ARTHUR AND STEVEN UPHAM

Tintype of Billy the Kid

could have a quick temper if pushed. He was good with firearms. He loved guns and took good care of his weapons. He was an excellent shot and reportedly "fast" on the draw. In legend Billy was a left-handed gunfighter. This misrepresentation surely came about because of the nature of tintypes. Billy posed for a picture in the summer of 1880 near Fort Summer. His very noticeable Colt was on his left side, which led observers to conclude that he was a southpaw. Tintypes, of course, are the reverse image of the subject so it's easy to see how the mistake was made. That reversed image could be a symbol for how being on the wrong side of a fight could take a scared kid and turn him into a notorious outlaw.

ANOTHER KID—HARVEY LOGAN, AKA KID CURRY

THE MOST WANTED, THE MOST DEADLY OUTLAW IN THE WEST?

Beneath Harvey Logan's apparent mild manner lurked an emotional volcano. Known to his friends as Kid Curry, the outlaw looked more like a nondescript store clerk than a killer. Perhaps five foot seven, he weighed around 150 pounds and had dark eyes, rich brown hair, a thick "waterfall" mustache, and a pudgy nose. There was no mistaking the confident way he moved or the sureness of his manner.

Farm life in Missouri proved too dull for Harvey Logan and his brothers. The romance of the West called. According to legend the adventurous young lads "borrowed" some horses and made their way to Wyoming, where they learned the finer points of cowboying and gun handling. Soon they were riding on the wrong side of the law.

The wayward life seemed to suit Harvey. He rode with Black Jack Ketchum and the Ketchum Gang, and after a disagreement with Ketchum, he fell in with the Wild Bunch and was a confidant of Butch Cassidy, the Sundance Kid, and Elza Lay.

Much has been made of the fast draw—it's the stuff of legend. Most gunfighters, men such as Wyatt Earp, Wild Bill Hickok, or Bat Masterson, for example, were excellent shots and cool under fire, but could not be considered "fast draws" by any stretch of the imagination. Kid Curry, however, was lightning with his six-gun. Unlike many who could clear leather quickly, but couldn't hit the broad side of a barn once they got the weapon into play, Curry was a deadly shot. In one town, stunned witnesses say he pulled and fired his Colt so fast it sounded like one shot—even though he fired several rounds. Few who fought him once got a second chance.

Curry had another edge when he was fighting. When he got mad, it didn't matter to him if he, or anyone else, lived or died. This cavalier attitude, when coupled with his natural speed and accuracy, made for a deadly combination and the stuff of the nonpareil gunslinger of Western legend. Among his associates, his good friend Butch Cassidy was one of the few men who could control him and calm him down.

In 1897 the Kid had his eye on a ripe plum, the Butte County Bank in Belle Fourche, South Dakota. The town was holding a big celebration for Civil War veterans, which meant a full vault and a lot of drinking and merrymaking. The outlaws hoped folks would have their guards down. Tom O'Day was assigned to go into town to look the place over, but he couldn't resist the watering holes and celebrations. He finally staggered back to camp with a king-sized hangover—having forgotten to collect the reconnaissance information they needed. He was lucky Curry didn't use him for target practice.

The next day Curry again sent O'Day in to look things over. Again, the thirsty Irishman couldn't get past the first saloon. Rumor has it he polished off two more bottles before his frustrated partners in crime rode in looking for him. They bungled the holdup, but managed to escape, barely. The bank job was a disaster and the take was very disappointing.

There was another side to Harvey Logan. He was faithful to his friends, and they were loyal to him. He was known for helping those who were down and out. He was well liked by many of the ranchers and cowboys in Wyoming and Montana, who felt he could do no wrong. The intelligent and observant Maud Davis, who was married to Wild Bunch outlaw Elza Lay said, "He was a gentleman clean through."

Regardless of what his friends said, it's the opinion of many historians that Harvey Logan, aka Kid Curry, was one of the most dangerous men in the West—at least, he is on nearly everyone's top-five list. Curry managed to earn one of the longest criminal records of his time. By the turn of the century, the rewards offered for this bold outlaw, wanted dead or alive, totaled more than forty thousand dollars, quite an extravagant figure.

Lowell Spence, a veteran Pinkerton agent who spent years on Curry's trail, was one of the few living lawmen who could be considered a first-hand expert on this slippery desperado. Spence said, "It was almost suicide to go after him. He wasn't the kind of man to run and hide; he would plot and plan and ambush you. After he escaped from Knoxville, I trailed him for months. It was a very tense time. I never knew when he would suddenly appear, gun in hand."

The Kid's luck ran out in June 1904 near Rifle, Colorado— or so some historians believe. Legend has it that Curry died like a romantic hero. He and some friends pulled a job, and a posse was soon on their tails. The most wanted outlaw in the West, Harvey Logan took a shot through his lungs and couldn't escape. He knew he was dying, so he told the others to go on while he held off the posse. Then, rather than be taken, he turned his trusty Colt on himself.

BUTCH CASSIDY AND THE SUNDANCE KID: A MYSTERIOUS ENDING

What really happened to the famous Wild Bunch outlaws Butch Cassidy and the Sundance Kid? Were they killed in Bolivia in one last, great shoot-out? Was their death a murder-suicide? Or did they escape and spend the rest of their lives in the United States under assumed names?

The situation looked hopeless for Butch and Sundance. Wounded but in good spirits, the two Robin Hood outlaws loaded up their Colt .45s, made a few jokes, strapped on extra ammunition belts, and courageously ran into approximately twenty thousand angry bullets fired by Bolivian troops. Thus two of the most successful outlaws in the Old West met their maker outside a dingy South American cantina.

But is that what really happened? The movie, *Butch Cassidy and the Sundance Kid*, portrays it that way. Opinions are divided—there are no bodies or smoking guns, so there is a lot of speculation. Many contemporary scholars feel that Butch and Sundance were, in fact, killed in San Vicente, Bolivia, in 1908. Indeed, there is some evidence that their deaths might have been a murder-suicide. Others, however, suggest the two clever banditos lived to a ripe old age, probably in the United States.

By 1900 the Old West had become a little too civilized, a little too hot, for the Wild Bunch. Their famous hideouts, Hole-in-the-Wall, Brown's Hole, and Robber's Roost, were no longer safe. Improved roads and telephones made escaping after a job difficult. And the Pinkerton Detective Agency and law officials had finally become dangerous threats. Butch Cassidy told his associates in crime that the law had become too acquainted with how they were doing business, and it was only a matter of time before they would be caught or worse, killed, if they continued business as usual, so in February of 1901, Butch Cassidy, the Sundance Kid, and Etta Place boarded a ship for South America. For a time they apparently tried living a quiet life on the Argentine pampas. They bought a large ranch in Patagonia at the foot of the Andes near the Chilean border, near Chubut, about 750 miles south of Buenos Aires. It was a lonely life among the sheep, cattle, and horses, but the land reminded Butch of his old stomping grounds in the American West (although the climate was milder). Both Cassidy and Sundance were excellent stockmen and their ranch prospered. Etta kept a neat house and was reportedly a good cook. There was a lot of rustling in southern Argentina, but whether or not the trio took up the practice is not known.

During the next four years, Sundance and Etta made several trips back to the United States. When Sundance and Etta left, the loneliness was almost too much for the gregarious Butch. He read whatever books he could get his hands on, worked hard, and visited ladies for hire. In Argentina and Bolivia women were apparently even more scarce than in the West, and only the larger towns had formal houses of prostitution. However, there were so-called "whores on wheels," girls (with strict, business-minded madams) who rode on big-wheeled carts that moved from rancho to rancho servicing the lonely *gaucho* clientele—often at the expense of the landowner. (Big ranchers discouraged their *gauchos* from getting married because they felt it caused contention among the ranks.)

It appears that on one occasion, he visited one girl too many and caught a nasty social disease. He cabled Sundance in America and told him to come back down to the ranch because he was so sore he couldn't get in a saddle for some time.

Because the trio was thousands of miles away from the United States, they didn't bother to hide the location of their rancho when they wrote letters to friends and family back home. What the outlaws didn't know was that the Pinkertons had bribed local postal employees to open up mail to family and known friends in order to learn the whereabouts of the outlaws. With evidence obtained through illegal mail tampering, the agency sent the surly detective Frank Dimaio to Buenos Aires to investigate.

By 1904 Butch and Sundance realized they had been a bit too careless with their correspondence; they'd have to move on. They were getting bored and restless with the quiet life anyway. They put the ranch up for sale, and it was purchased by an Englishman who managed a number of other local ranchos. As they left Argentina, they robbed the Banco de Tarapaca after closing out their accounts. They made a good haul, too, possibly the equivalent of one hundred thousand dollars today.

They hit a number of other banks; all the robberies were well planned with Butch's usual precision. There is evidence that Etta dressed up, strapped on a six-shooter, and joined the boys in the robbery. But sometime around 1906 Etta left South America. Sundance may have gone with her, but he returned to South America alone. Some speculate that she went to Denver to have her appendix removed and later died. Others wonder if she needed serious treatment for a venereal disease, had an abortion, or delivered a baby. Maybe the political climate was getting tenuous because of their crimes and her lover wanted to remove her from danger. It is also possible that she and Sundance simply called it quits. We simply don't know.

After her departure Butch and Sundance continued to do well in South America, but things were starting to heat up—thanks to their crime spree.

In 1906 or 1907 the pair decided to let the situation cool off a bit. They took jobs at the Concordia Tin Mines at Tres Cruces in Bolivia—about one hundred miles from La Paz. The two American outlaws were considered outstanding employees and continually pleased their employers with their hard work. Ironically, they helped guard the payrolls from bandits. No one robbed the money during their watch. Neither Butch nor Sundance would think of stealing from an outfit they worked for—they had a code of ethics, after all. Their bosses said they were honest to a fault and did a good day's work for a day's pay. The two finally told their employers about their past profession, but that didn't seem to matter. On one occasion Butch found out that there was a plot to kidnap one of the mine officials, so he arranged for his protection.

By 1908 the outlaws had given notice to Concordia and gone back to their old profession full time—being company men was too dull. They made themselves quite unpopular with train officials, mining management, and law enforcement, pulling off some big scores and hiding in the Andes while the heat was on.

Evidently two bandits—we're not absolutely sure if they were Butch and Sundance—couldn't resist the temptation of a rather large payroll from the Aramayo, Francke, & Cia Mining Company. With bandanas covering their faces, Colts in hand, they robbed the mule train carrying the loot near Tupiza, Bolivia. They fled into the rugged mountains, but two days later found themselves in the Bolivian town of San Vicente. What happened there, and how it happened, is still open to some debate.

If this was, indeed, his gig, Butch, got careless. Normally he would have been more careful, camping in the bush for a time and watching the back trail—letting things cool off before heading to a town, even a small one. But the banditos got anxious for a bed and a meal and rode for civilization. The two were well armed, which drew some attention to them. Then, as fortune would have it, they inadvertently asked a local policeman where they could stay. Not knowing that he was talking to two of the most wanted men in the Andes, he directed them to a local inn. The two weary Americans unloaded their mules and supplies in the courtyard and ordered food.

The policeman apparently recognized some of the mules—they belonged to a good friend who worked for one of the senior Aramayo Mine officials. The policeman also knew the mine payroll had been robbed by two well-armed Yankees. The gendarme knew he wasn't brave enough to approach them by himself. However, as it happened, a group of soldiers was camped outside of town. The local man sent word to the officer in charge and asked for help. Before long soldiers had taken positions around the cantina.

Anxious to make a name for himself, the captain came in person to demand their surrender. A gun battle of some intensity ensued.

From here the story gets crazy. The battle might have lasted all night, an hour, or five minutes. The outlaws had their Colts, but apparently had left their rifles outside. Some say that the Kid took a bullet when he tried for the long guns at the pack, and Butch dragged him back into the cantina. No one is sure. Others proposed from forensic evidence (assuming the skulls in question were those of the two outlaws), that when the situation was hopeless, Butch probably shot his partner and used the last round on himself, so he wouldn't be taken alive.

Two men were killed in this gunfight and buried in an Indian cemetery close by. But were they Butch and Sundance? One local tradition suggests that at least one of the dead men was a Chilean, not an American. Remigio Sanchez, who supposedly saw the battle and its results, claimed that one of the men was wounded in the temple and the other had several bullet wounds in his arm. The mine's payroll was found among the dead men's belongings—as well as money from a previous robbery. Some accounts say the soldiers also found medicine and a famous Tiffany watch, possibly the one Etta used to wear, on the men. Neither the soldiers nor the police identified the bodies very carefully. The mine got the payroll back and the men were dead—that's all that really mattered at the time.

For a while there was a fair amount of skepticism about the shooting, but it started to become gradually accepted that Butch and Sundance had been killed at San Vicente. South American newspaper stories—even less reliable than American papers of the same period—told how two Yankee bandits had met their sad end. Although many of the circumstances in the accounts were contradictory, American officials at La Paz were reasonably certain that at least one of the dead men was a Wild Bunch member. But for many people, questions about the outlaws' fate remained. There were too many holes in the story and too many rumors of their return.

Were Butch and Sundance at San Vicente at all? Could Butch and Sundance have somehow switched places with other men at the last minute and escaped? Were they able to bribe someone and get out of the hacienda before the shooting was over? Could someone else have dressed up in their clothes before or after they were shot? Was this one of Butch's plans to keep the South American authorities off his trail? Could the two dead men be another pair of outlaws known to be working in the area? If the dead men were other outlaws, did Butch and Sundance take advantage of a fortuitous situation and plan a hasty retirement? There are a lot of might-haves that keep the story alive in folklore.

As late as the 1920s, the Pinkerton Detective Agency still assumed the outlaws were living in South America, and the files on Cassidy and Sundance were considered active. There is no authoritative record in Pinkerton accounts suggesting the two men had been killed.

It's true that letters to friends and family stopped almost instantly, but there might be reasonable explanations for this. The men might have figured out that their mail was no longer safe, since it was obvious their letters were being read by detectives. Further, how do we explain the number of unrelated, but seemingly credible, Butch and Sundance sightings and visits that took place after the shooting? In Sundance's family, most believe he died in Bolivia, but not all. Some of Butch's kin tell of many family visits, occurring after his supposed death. A number of his friends from the Wild Bunch days also say he visited them after San Vicente.

Butch's sister says that around 1925 the family was astonished when Robert LeRoy Parker (Butch's real name) arrived at the family ranch for a visit. The family had nearly given him up for dead. They drove back to town where Butch visited with his father, then in his eighties, and several of his brothers. Butch is supposed to have said that it took him so long to come back because he was ashamed of what he had done, and that he spent a good deal of time in Mexico, where Sundance and Etta were living.

When his brothers and sisters asked him about the shoot-out in Bolivia, he said he'd learned more about it since coming back to the United States than he learned down south—implying he wasn't there. He said a good friend in Bolivia, Percy Seibert, had told officials the dead bodies were his and Sundance's, hoping to give his friends a second chance. Butch told his family that he'd been to Europe and Alaska in his travels. He was now making the Pacific Northwest his home.

The Parker family agreed to keep their wayward brother's visit a family secret, so they could protect him. If asked, they said that he was dead. It wasn't until the 1970s that Lula broke the "family silence" in *Butch Cassidy, My Brother.*

The book sold well, but met with mixed reviews. Even though by then Butch was long dead, many members of her family didn't appreciate the book because it broke a promise. The Parker family didn't back her up on all the incidents she reported, and some scholars also took Lula to task for not being direct about where and how her brother died. Some of her stories and tales are flimsy, loosely connected, fabricated tales. Despite the book's flaws, it is a fun read and a wonderful piece of folklore.

Butch is reported to have visited both of the Bassett sisters from Brown's Hole—long-time friends from the Wild Bunch glory days—on several occasions. Both women were confidential about the visits until later, when it didn't matter. Ann Bassett Willis and her husband Frank Willis said they had a reunion with the Wild Bunch leader at Butch's cabin in Nevada, among other places. Josie Bassett McNight told of several visits. Her daughter-in-law Edith, who supposedly met the famous outlaw, said in a 1973 interview, "If you ever got a look at his eyes, you'd never forget those eyes."

Matt Warner, a famous outlaw turned lawman and former member of the Wild Bunch, was a close friend of both Butch and Sundance. In his biography Warner tells his readers that he didn't see Butch or Sundance after they left for South America—suggesting they were killed in Bolivia. Some argue he would go to great lengths to protect his two Wild Bunch friends because he hints elsewhere that he met his old friends in some clandestine way after they'd returned from South America. There is no way of knowing for sure. At any rate Joyce Warner, his daughter, implies that her father visited with one or both of his outlaw friends in his old age. Joyce also insinuates, although there is no proof, that she got mail from Butch before the beginning of World War II.

Tom Vernon of Baggs, Wyoming, said that Butch visited him around the same time that he visited his sister Lula. On one of his trips to Wyoming, Butch apparently reunited with his old outlaw friend Elza Lay. We'll never know if the tales of Butch sightings are true. One thing is certain: None of Butch's friends would have thought twice about lying to protect him if he truly did visit them. Butch inspired a rare loyalty among his associates. To make it more confusing, and to fuel the Butch sightings phenomenon, there were fake "Butches" who went about pretending to be the old outlaw. The so-called fake Butches could fool an acquaintance, but it seems unlikely that such a fraud would fool an old friend for long.

Another widely circulated story says Butch spent the rest of his life as a Spokane, Washington, businessman named Phillips, who died in the late 1930s. This argument convinces some, but others feel that Phillips was one of the Butch impersonators.

Two excellent Wild Bunch researchers, Dan Buck and Anne Meadows, argued that this mystery could be laid to rest with DNA samples from the gravesites in San Vicente. PBS's *Nova* thought it would be an interesting study, too, and decided to do a documentary about their expedition. With a camera crew and a team of experts, they went to the village and visited the Bolivian cemetery.

San Vicente is still quite remote. From the capital they rode a rickety train for fifteen hours. Then they spent four bone-jarring hours in a four-wheel-drive vehicle, creeping over steep mountain roads until they arrived at their destination. The researchers were pretty sure they knew where to look, and with the cooperation of the Bolivian government, the bodies in question were exhumed. The physical anthropologist on hand to assist them at the site determined that the remains looked to be Caucasian and of the appropriate size. There were also metal stains on the remains that might suggest possible bullet wounds, but the bodies were too old to make a definitive determination. There were interesting boot remnants, a partial sole and leather fragments, indicating one of the men had small feet—supposedly a Sundance Kid attribute.

The team had permission to take the bones back to Oklahoma where more comprehensive scientific analysis could be performed. In the lab it was determined that there were, indeed, metal shards in one of the skulls, indicating a bullet wound. There was also evidence to indicate that one of the men might have had an old leg wound caused by a bullet—supposedly the Kid did take a slug in his leg at one time.

The next test was the most important—a DNA investigation that would make or break the researchers' theory. When DNA from the remains and from known Butch and Sundance relatives were compared, neither set matched up. The remains, after all, were not the two outlaws in question.

In spite of the setback, Buck and Meadows are still convinced, justifiably, that Butch and Sundance were buried in the graveyard. They believe that they simply dug up the wrong graves. They argue, along with others in their camp, that even without the DNA proof, it seems logical the men died in San Vicente. Letters to family and friends in both North and South America stopped at this time. The robbery followed Butch's modus operandi. The men also fit Butch and Sundance's descriptions and there were identifying personal effects on the bodies. A friend named Percy Seibert may also have been on hand to name them or identify the bodies (accounts differ).

However, unless conclusive DNA evidence is found, it's conceivable that the two men escaped and managed to make their way back into the United States—or that they weren't in

Butch Cassidy

the shoot-out at all. This thinking doesn't stem from a patriotic notion that Butch and Sundance, two noble American bad guys, couldn't be killed. The truth is most bandits in that region were caught by police and soldiers before long—and many of those bandits were from the US.

And so the myth of Butch and Sundance lives on!

Harry Longabaugh (aka The Sundance Kid) and Etta Place

ETTA PLACE: MYSTERY WOMAN

Etta Place had long, thick hair, intelligent, deep-brown eyes, an alluring smile, a calming voice, and a pleasant personality. She was on the small side, rather shapely, and quick-witted, as well. The story of Etta Place and her association with the Wild Bunch has been cobbled together from folklore, hearsay, and history. At the heart of the myth surrounding the gorgeous mystery woman are some fundamental questions: Who was she really, and why did she take up with outlaws?

Everyone agrees that Etta Place was the Sundance Kid's companion. She was reputed to be an excellent rider and an excellent shot with a rifle. Etta Place probably wasn't her real name. At different times she may have gone by Ethel, Eva, or Eunice. Her real last name might have been Ingerfield, Capel, or Thayne, among other possibilities. Frank Dimaio, a seasoned Pinkerton detective, believed that Etta was a working girl from Fanny Porter's Sporting House. It is possible that Butch may have found her and rescued her from that sordid life. We know Butch probably bailed out several girls who wanted to go home and quit the business.

Other historians think they may have connected Etta to the Parkers in Utah (Butch's family—his real name was Robert LeRoy Parker). They feel that she was actually one of Butch's cousins. She and Butch would have known each other as children and been reacquainted as adults.

One of the more interesting theories about Etta Place is that she was Ann Bassett, the Queen of the Rustlers, who hailed from Brown's Hole in northwestern Colorado—a haven for rustlers and some of the West's most wanted outlaws—and was quite possibly a silent partner in Butch Cassidy's outlaw career. Ann could ride and shoot as well as most men and had a reputation as a woman who could not be tamed. Robbery and rustling wouldn't have bothered her—nor would "living in sin."

The theory that the women were one and the same gained credibility in the 1990s. Existing photos of Ann Bassett and Etta Place were compared using computer analysis, and initial tests showed there was only a one-in-five-thousand chance that Etta and Ann were two different women. A further test revealed a barely noticeable scar on Ann's forehead. Etta's photo is supposed to have the same scar.

Historians have tried to corroborate the photo evidence by comparing dates when Ann left her ranch with the times Etta was known to be with Butch or Sundance. Most interesting was the fall of 1900; when Ann left her home for a vacation, Etta showed up in Texas visiting Sundance. A short time later, in February of 1901, Ann again left her home. According to Pinkerton records, Etta, Butch, and Sundance returned to the United States from South America in July 1902. Before the end of the summer, the absent Ann was back at her ranch in Brown's Hole.

Reputable scholars, however, are not convinced that Ann was Etta Place. It's a fun story, but hardly credible. The evidence is too conflicting. For example, on the day that Etta was supposed to have docked in New York on her return from South America, Ann was seen in Colorado. Additionally there are letters with postmarks to family and friends that indicate Ann's vacation was in the United States.

Around 1907 Etta slipped out of Western history and into legend. Speculation about her past and her eventual fate leads to some intriguing possibilities. One theory has Etta as a madam who operated a successful brothel in Fort Worth, Texas, where she lived until 1962 when she died in a hotel fire. Richard Llewellyn, the author of *How Green Was My Valley*, felt the elusive Etta lived in Argentina, later moving to Paraguay where she married a government official. Another rumor has her involved with a boxing promoter from Texas who ran a large South American ranch.

Others say Sundance checked her into a Denver hospital and walked away, never to return. Some report she died before (or during) an operation. There's no record in any hospital of a woman who fits her description.

Butch's sister, Lula Parker Betenson, tells us that when Butch came to visit her in the 1920s, he had previously visited Sundance and Etta in Mexico City, where the two were living. There is also some evidence that a woman fitting Etta's description tried in 1911 or 1912 to get a death certificate for one of the outlaws killed in New Mexico. The truth is we just don't know.

BUFFALO:
THE EXTERMINATION ORDER

Why couldn't buffalo and civilization coexist? How did the herds disappear so quickly? Why was the extermination of the buffalo a political move in a larger chess game? And, did some microbe, introduced by domestic cattle, play a final role in the demise of the buffalo?

The word *bison* is the proper scientific term for the magnificent beast that once roamed the US in vast herds—but we don't care. *Buffalo* incites images of the Wild West, the Great Prairies, and the promise of a frontier. These animals are, it seems, the terrible and wonderful gift of a mythological demigod and the root of American folklore. The charge of a stampeding herd, for example, must sound like "rolling thunder" because buffalo have always seemed larger than life. When the first Europeans set foot in the New World, buffalo ranged from Canada to Mexico, from the tidal waters of Virginia and Georgia to the edges of the Great Basin. The epicenter, of course, was the Great Plains. The population was estimated at 60 to 70 million animals.

Always moving in search of better grazing, this free-ranging prairie-grazing machine was not easily corralled. It was tough and bold and reckless and obtuse—much like our pioneer stock. Building a new country, after all, is very hard work. We did wonderful things in our first century of democracy, but we made mistakes, too. We came close to losing a rare natural resource, and we did it on purpose. The buffalo was not "simply" overhunted for hides, meat, or sport: It was carefully exterminated.

Meriwether Lewis observed in August of 1806: "The [buffalo] are so numerous that . . . if it be not impossible to calculate the moving multitude, which darkened the whole plain . . . we are convinced that twenty-thousand would be no exaggerated number." To the first observers, the herds seemed to stretch into infinity and were as endless as the land itself. Coronado in the 1540s, exploring what is now the Texas Panhandle, said the bison "were so vast that I did not reach the end although I marched over them for a 1,000 miles." The Corps of Discovery was in awe of the great herds. The expedition, though, got a "bison lesson" that served as a proverbial wakeup call. A lone animal ripped into camp after dark and the consequences could have been disastrous. Apparently disoriented, the beast charged through the beached boats and nearly trampled the campfire. Its deadly hooves missed the heads of sleeping men by inches. It happened so fast the guards were not able to shout an alarm.

This incident foreshadows one of the great problems: Buffalo do not "play" well with others and can be dangerous. Evidence of this fact can be found in modern-day Yellowstone National Park, where these animals top the list for injuries and fatalities suffered by park visitors. Buffalo run three to four times faster than humans and they go where they want. They are unpredictable and, while loveable, they're not very bright. They are herd animals, after all. Blindly "following the leader" is in their DNA. One of the great fears—a justified fear, I might add—on the Great Plains was of getting caught in a stampede. Buffalo weren't respectful of human beings, human ingenuity, or human machinations (fences, ranches, farms, houses, watersheds, livestock, railroads, or wagon trains).

Although the animal is very killable with a firearm or a bow (especially if one is mounted on a horse), a long list of Native Americans, experienced plainsmen, buffalo hunters, and greenhorns have entered into the next life via "buffalo miscalculation." A good postulate for right-of-way issues: yield! A bull can stand six and a half feet tall from hump to hoof, weigh two thousand pounds, and measure twelve feet long from nose to tail tip. Getting trampled was a real concern in buffalo country. Getting a few shots off might kill a few lead animals, but more would be following right behind.

Catherine Haun, a young bride on the Oregon Trail in 1849, recorded the following observation: "The herd came like a great black cloud. The people watched as thousands of buffalo raced straight toward their wagon train about 35 miles an hour. The earth trembled beneath the thundering hooves. The buffalo could not be turned aside, and there was not time to escape . . . leaving people trampled and injured."

In 1856, a company of Latter-day Saint "handcart" pioneers felt they had been miraculously spared. Their goal was Zion in the Great Basin. They became surrounded by a rather large herd of bison one day in the fall. At first this seemed like a good thing because they were running low on provisions and desperately needed protein. Although they only had a few buffalo rifles, the Saints could almost taste the fresh haunches roasting over a chip fire. The mood of the party changed rapidly, however, from eager anticipation to terror. The animals started and stampeded. The chaotic charge ran off livestock, upset handcarts, and scattered personal property across the prairie. By frontier standards, those pioneers got off easily.

Around this same time period, a journalist from Wood River Center in Kansas wrote, "Our beautiful town site has been rudely trampled by those ugly-looking wild beasts known as buffalo." An observer on the Overland Trail noted, "Progress was retarded by herds of buffalo which lined the roads." In 1859, Horace Greeley reported, "All we saw could not have stood on ten square miles of ground . . . the country for miles seemed black with them."

Considering the current focus on preserving the much-reduced population of buffalo, it seems odd nowadays that the likes of Buffalo Bill, who made his reputation killing buffalo, would be so admired. In our modern comforts, we must remember that plains travel was dangerous. At least 10 percent of the settlers would not survive the trail and were mostly buried in unmarked graves (numbering in the tens of thousands). Disease, accidents, and starvation took a wicked toll. Indians were feared and buffalo (like grizzly) were fun to read about in pulp fiction but difficult to live with when they affected your living or your personal safety. Buffalo Bill was not killing for fun, he was shooting for money—he was a well-paid market hunter, hired to provide meat.

The buffalo was a short-term answer for a pressing problem as the country expanded west. While often a hazardous nuisance, these shaggy beasts were four-legged food and clothing for settlers, farmers and ranchers, and empire builders (rail workers and miners) as they passed through the Great Plains to the promised land of their choice. These prairie beasts were relatively easy to hunt, their meat was delicious, and the hides made clothing that would stand up to a prairie blizzard or a Rocky Mountain winter. With the crash of the beaver market in the 1830s, many unemployed trappers turned to buffalo hunting. This animal was a "low-hanging fruit" to be exploited. As beaver prices crashed, a decade or two before the great human migrations, the demand for buffalo hides and capes increased in both American and European markets. As early as 1825–1830 the buffalo became a "cash crop" for trappers and Native Americans. During this five-year period more than 130,000 hides were shipped by flat boats to New Orleans. A case in point would be the Blackfeet Indians, who were the reigning lords of the Northern Plains before smallpox nearly wiped out their numbers. Cunning businessmen, the Blackfeet held a virtual monopoly on trade, supplying tens of thousands of hides for trade goods.

By the 1840s, traffic on the eastern leg of the Overland Trail (from Kansas to Wyoming) had caused the buffalo to split into northern and southern herds. This became more noticeable during the California Gold Rush when hundreds of thousands of settlers further interrupted traditional migration patterns.

Until the 1850s, the Great Plains were an obstacle to be crossed to get to someplace better. (The land, in theory, was supposed to be held in trust for the indigenous peoples.) However, when the prairie became "the promised land," enough was enough. Buffalo became more than a commercial venture or a traveler's nuisance—the herds had become obstacles. In the name of progress, the buffalo had to go from the plains of Kansas, Nebraska, Colorado, Texas, the Black Hills, and other lesser-known places.

After the Civil War, change was rapid. As the Great Plains, the so-called "American Desert," became a destination for settlers, the Plains tribes became another obstacle. The scorched-earth policy that had worked for the Union Army in the recent war was adopted by the US Army. Soldiers were ordered to attack the enemy and attack the supply lines—in this case, the buffalo. As Colonel Dodge commented, "Every buffalo dead is an Indian gone." James Throckmorton, a Texas congressman, said, "It would be a great step forward in the civilization of the Indians and the preservation of peace on the border if there was not a buffalo in existence." In the name of peace on the Plains, the buffalo had to go. As long as the tribes relied on this food source, they would never move to reservations.

Today we wonder how our forefathers could fail to appreciate that the bison herds were among the greatest on earth—or that they could be wiped out so quickly. By the 1870s millions and millions of hides had been transported by rail alone to Eastern cities. Precisely how many millions were killed is unknown. Yes, we had developed a taste for salted buffalo tongues and buffalo coats. Yes, buffalo bones could be made into great fertilizer (five thousand rail cars a year, stuffed with bones and skulls, made their way to Eastern grinding mills). Yes, buffalo hunts were in fashion.

But the decimation of these vast herds happened so quickly that it took the nation by surprise. In the 1870s there were millions of buffalo. By the mid-1880s they were mostly gone. Lewis and Clark, keen naturalists, would have been incredulous had they foreseen what children born at the time of their expedition would live to see. Of course, we were good at killing, but not that good. It was a perfect storm for species annihilation. We also got help from microbes and climate change.

1874 illustration titled "Slaughtered for the Hide"

BUFFALO: THE OTHER FACTORS

Market hunting and shooting were major factors that greatly reduced the buffalo populations among already stressed herds. However, there were other factors to consider, including loss of habitat, climate change, more-than-subsistence hunting by native populations, and disease.

1. Loss of habitat and competition from livestock were critical problems for buffalo. The native herds suddenly had no place to go. Valleys that had been traditional homelands for buffalo became populated with people, agriculture, and livestock, so the forage was gone. Cattle and horse herds were competing for grazing.

2. Population numbers have always been affected by climate changes, but when the numbers are already in a serious decline, the effects can be serious. Droughts in the 1840s and 1850s had taken their toll on herd numbers. Horrific blizzards on the Plains in the early 1880s took their toll, as well.

3. Another factor in the decline of the buffalo is that Native American populations were killing more animals than they needed for food. Hides were used for trade goods after the 1820s. By the 1850s some estimates suggest that Native Americans were killing close to five hundred thousand animals a year—certainly more animals than they could use for food—then taking the hides and leaving behind carcasses to rot. Certainly those numbers are nothing compared to later kill rates, but the numbers start to add up as early as the 1830s.

4. Did domestic cattle play another role? Buffalo were still counted in the millions in the late 1870s . . . and yet they seemed to disappear in just a few years. While the outcome was near extinction by the mid- to late 1880s, and we're taught that the

buffalo herds were hunted to the brink of extinction, it's a little more complicated than that. There is an interesting thesis discussed among some historians and scholars that perhaps a virus, loosely referred to as "tick fever" or "Texas fever," caused the final destruction of the northern herd (the southern herd was mostly gone at this point).

Any of several diseases may have been contributing factors in the decimation of the great herds, but since veterinary medicine was still in its infancy, it's difficult to ascertain what role these diseases may have played. However, in mid-1800s, some sort of virus had destructive effects on herd populations. In what is now eastern Nebraska, nearly all of the buffalo died off quickly in the 1840s. The same thing happened in eastern Wyoming as the result of a regionalized buffalo version of the plague. While the drop in buffalo numbers was alarming to subsistence hunters, and surprising to plainsmen, the overall population was sustainable and within a few years had recovered.

GRIZZLY BEARS: BEYOND THE TALL TALE

Is the ferocity of the grizzly a tall tale? Is it campfire talk about a creature that nearly passed into the legendary West? Are these bears as aggressive and moody and as dangerous and hard to kill as we read in Western literature? Is the temperament of the grizzly really that different from a black bear?

It's called *Ursus horribilis* for cause.

Jedediah Smith was no greenhorn, yet for the rest of his life he would wear his hair long to cover the missing ear, the missing eyebrow, and the nasty scar across his head. In the Old West, you learned fast or you died—few mountain men reached old age.

In the fall of 1823, Smith was leading a party of mountain men on the South Fork of the Cheyenne River in what is now the Black Hills of South Dakota. The stream was brush-choked when Smith and the bear came face-to-face. The attack was unprovoked. It just happened. James Clyman was an eyewitness to one of the most famous grizzly events in history. He recorded it in his diary. He notes how the bear suddenly attacked. It hit Smith headfirst and flipped him to the ground: "Grissly did not hesitate a moment but sprung on the cap[t] taking him by the head first pitc[hing] sprawling on the earth . . . he gave him a grab by the middle . . . breaking his ribs."

As often happens in a close-quarters attack, the charge is explosive and over almost as soon as it begins. A head attack is especially dangerous. An adult bear's bite has a force of around nine hundred pounds per square inch (more powerful than an African lion or a great white shark). A grizzly can break a six-inch pine tree in one snap of its jaws. The silvertip that grabbed Smith by the head should have killed him. Jedediah was not a small man, yet this bear tossed him about like a rag. As soon as Smith was on the ground, the bruin went for his chest. What saved Smith was the knife and sack of lead rounds on his belt. In all fairness, the bear's bite broke the knife in two, but that apparently discouraged further attacks. Smith was lucky the angry animal didn't swat him. A large grizzly can turn over a five-hundred-pound dumpster. As the saying goes, there's power in "them paws." One blow can break a moose's neck.

When the attack was over, the bear ran off without a shot being fired. Apparently Smith was not only a stoic mountain man, he was also God-fearing. He comforted himself by reciting the Twenty-third Psalm over and over: "Though I walk through the valley of the shadow of death, I will fear no evil." He was glad to be alive—although his day was surely ruined and he needed comforting. He was a bloody mess when his men got to him. Ostensibly in shock, but thinking clearly for a moment, he told them to fetch water and clean him up. He instructed that someone should take a needle and thread and "stich" him up. He reportedly didn't move—the psalm helped. The sewing up, of course, was more easily said than done since half his scalp had ripped off and was flapping uselessly. Using a harness needle and saddle thread from his kit, Clyman did the best he could to patch Smith back together. As

Clyman wrote, "I [found] the bear had tak nearly all his head in his mouth close to his left eye on one side an clos [close] to his right ear . . . and laid the skull bare near the crown."

Smith was a tough man. After resting for a few weeks, he led his party to the Wind River Valley. But there were more bears in his future. Before the colorful Smith met his end on the Cimarron River in Southwest Kansas as a result of an Indian attack, grizzlies would give him a few more chances to even the score. One time was on Antelope Creek in Northern California. A silvertip charged from a thicket and grabbed the tail and rump of the horse Smith was riding. Smith said the bear hung on for more than fifty yards before it lost its grasp. A few days later, in the same drainage, Smith dodged another attack by diving into a deep pool in Antelope Creek when a grizzly charged.

In the spring of 1805, the Lewis and Clark Expedition left Fort Mandan after their first winter. They were understandably anxious about the trip, and their journals express some fear about the great bears they would encounter. The Mandan warriors warned that the great bear would attack more often than not. The braves only hunted the bears in large groups, and, as they would when they went to war, they wore war paint. Lewis observed, "They [would] paint themselves and perform all the superstitious rights commonly observed when [they] are about to make war." So awesome was the bear's prowess that it was the cause of death for many warriors. Hunting a bear was taken seriously and lives often were lost in the process.

The plains grizzly, which the Corps of Discovery would soon encounter, "would be the size of common ox" and "intimidates us all." On the morning of April 29, 1805, along the Yellowstone River (in present-day Montana), members of the expedition shot their first grizzlies. They wounded both bears. One ran off, while the other very wounded bear charged Lewis. It pursued him for "seventy or eighty yards" so he could not reload. The others were able to kill it. The bear was not a mature bear, estimated at three hundred pounds. The Corps of Discovery got a lesson in great bears. As they were beginning to discover, the grizzly was not a creature to be taken lightly.

About a week later, Lewis and interpreter George Drouillard were about to get more grizzly education. Nearly fifty miles up the Yellowstone River, Lewis and Drouillard were out for an evening stroll when they saw another bear that would prove "extremely hard to kill." They put five rounds through its lungs and another five balls in other vitals. Fortunately for the men, the bear swam a half-mile to an island, and then it took twenty more minutes to die. The men realized that this wasn't your average black bear. This bear was a little over eight feet from nose to tail—not extremely large for a grizzly, but nearly twice the length of the average black bear.

In 1806, not far from Lolo Pass, Montana, Lewis would later record, "A hunter separated from his horse had a one in ten chance of escaping a grizzly attack." The men hunted grizzlies in groups and felt that head shots were the best bet since a bear, especially a grizzly, can eat a lot of lead. They had developed a very healthy respect for the great bears in a short time.

Mountain men often killed bears in self-defense. They also found the 36-caliber Kentucky-style long rifles didn't carry a large enough piece of lead or have enough power to do the job. The demands of the Plains and the western mountains required a more powerful rifle of 45 to 50 caliber.

Even the most experienced mountain man can get careless—even if he's loaded for bear. Isaac Slover, for example, had trapped from the Arkansas River to Santa Fe. He had wandered over what is now the Colorado Rockies and settled in San Bernardino, California, for the easy life. (The state of California had ten thousand grizzlies—which is a lot of teeth and claws.) In October, Slover was hunting the brushy oak country near Cajon Pass when he encountered a grizzly. He would have been using a big-bore muzzle loader, 50 caliber or better (the lead ball would be three times heavier than the average bullet used in a deer rifle). Maybe his shot wasn't as true as he'd hoped or this was a tough bear with attitude. We know he had time to reload (a process that takes over half a minute and could feel like an eternity if the bear were charging). He just got sloppy. The undergrowth was thick, and as he approached, he was likely overly confident that the bear was dead. Supposedly "dead" bears are the ones that get you, and this one did. According to his hunting buddy, a guy named McMines, the "bear gave a sudden spring" and ripped the hunter to shreds. They got the gravely wounded man "off the mountain" before he died. His head was opened like cheap wrapping paper and he suffered from broken legs and a broken arm—and some uncertain internal injuries.

Among the long list of grizzly attack casualties, some were careless, others were unlucky, and many were never named but simply labeled "missing in the West." Lewis Dawson, for example, was killed by a grizzly near Purgatory Creek in Colorado in 1821. So was Andrew Sublette, who was killed in Malibu Canyon, near

Santa Monica, California. And Hugh Glass, the famous mountain man, was mauled and miraculously survived after a horrific ordeal. The list goes on.

George Yount, a noted mountain man from frontier legend, said of the beasts, "They were everywhere—upon the plains, in the valleys, and on the mountains, venturing even into camping grounds. . . . I've often killed five or six in one day . . . and see[n] fifty or sixty in twenty-four hours." Certainly Yount was uttering his western version of the epic boast, but his point was that there were a lot of bears. Winter, Indians, disease, and bears were the great equalizers among mountain men.

Brad Treat wasn't as lucky as some others. When he rounded a corner on Halfmoon Trail, he couldn't know he would measure the rest of his life in panicked breaths. He would be dead in less than a minute. A grizzly came out of nowhere, not unlike the bear that attacked Smith, and knocked him down. And then for Treat it was all over. It was a warm day for the Montana country west of the Divide. There were a few clouds in the sky and the temperature was in the 80s. It was a lousy day to die.

It didn't matter why because dead is dead—at least for Brad Treat. There might have been a logical reason for the attack, but often a grizzly has an aggressive nature and that's simply how it is when you live in bear country. Unlike Jedediah Smith, almost two hundred years earlier, Brad Treat was a modern-day mountain man. He wasn't carrying a muzzleloader or trapping beaver. He was on a mountain bike in the Flathead National Forest not far from his home and just miles from the west entrance of Glacier National Park. He was no pilgrim or bleary-eyed tenderfoot. He'd lived in grizzly country most of his life. He'd been a park ranger for twelve years and was currently a law enforcement officer for the Forest Service. He was out for a ride with a relative. He knew bears, but it's the bears you don't see . . . or that you see too late.

Brad's death caught the headlines, unlike so many others who simply disappeared. In fact, Brad Treat's death occurred, ironically, on June 27, 2016, while I was writing about Jedediah Smith. Nothing has changed much in grizzly country since Lewis and Clark—except that there are fewer grizzlies and we've tamed too much wilderness.

While black bears are dangerous animals, only rarely do they go rogue and pose a threat to humans. Grizzly bears, on the other hand, should always be considered a threat. This bear is dangerous, moody, and temperamental. It has an aggressive nature and has never been intimidated by humans.

At the same time, the grizzly or brown bear is also wondrous, beautiful, and haunting—a true symbol of the West and wilderness. It's also one of the great success stories of modern-day conservation. We nearly lost the grizzly in the continental United States. Now I'm happy to report that there are sustainable populations in the lower forty-eight. These occur in the Greater Yellowstone Ecosystem and in the northern Rockies (although this represents only on a fraction of the bear's traditional homeland). The population below the Canadian border is over one thousand animals.

From 2010 to 2015 there were at least eighteen fatal bear attacks in the United States and Canada—eleven of these attacks were from grizzly bears. How many close calls, how many bears were turned by warning gunshots or bear spray, is impossible to tell. You only become a statistic if you're killed or mauled. The number of bears that are killed in self-defense, but unreported, is not quantifiable.

It would be wrong to assume that all bear attacks are provoked by humans. Attacks are considered defensive or predatory. But again, that's too easy. Having spent nearly four thousand days out of doors in bear country as a historian and an outdoor journalist, seven hundred of those days actively seeking bear populations, I sometimes wonder if bears aren't sure of what they're doing until they do it.

Certainly, stumbling into a sow with cubs, walking onto a food cache, running away, or violating a bear's space, especially a grizzly bear, produces predicable behavior. But as a photographer, I've slipped within yards of bears without incident.

Remember, there are close to one million black bears in the United States; only a few states don't have populations. While occasionally a nuisance, black bear numbers are exploding. There may be more black bears today than when Lewis and Clark explored the West. The bears I stumbled too close to, the bears I didn't know about, were scenarios that cause concern. And sometimes, for whatever reason, bears—black bears included—are predatory. This is the most dangerous of situations. Hunger or age might turn a bear predatory, but as often as not, there is no apparent reason. Animals have personalities just as people do. For the mountain men and those trying to make a living or carve out a homeland in the West, grizzly bears were one of the very real dangers. There were fifty to one hundred thousand grizzlies at the time of Lewis and Clark, from the Great Plains to Texas to California.

Bear legends are certainly steeped in hyperbole, but the kernel of the story has not changed. While both black and grizzly bears have killed humans, and still do, grizzly attacks are still the stuff of nightmares. In 2014 a 375-pound grizzly bear in Yukon Territories, near Whitehorse, busted through a picture window in the family cabin. Although she fought back, the bear dragged Claudia Huber out of the house and across a small creek. It did not end well. The bear ignored the barking dog, and investigating authorities said the family had done nothing to attract the bear.

Due to overhunting and habitat loss, the great bear nearly disappeared into legend. Thankfully, we've preserved some wilderness where the bear can live alongside us in some kind of truce.

BEAR FACTS

You can't outrun a bear—don't try. It's impossible and it will surely make matters worse, as it will trigger a chase. A football player is considered fast if he can run 18 miles per hour (roughly 26 feet per second). A grizzly bear can run 30 to 35 mph (or more than 40 feet per second). Here's an interesting statistic: In forty-two documented accounts of people running from bears in Alaska, in thirty-eight of those cases the bears chased and injured the person.

You can't dodge a bear, either. When a bear runs it seems to float over forest and prairie and brush—they make a cutting horse look clumsy.

A bear can run the length of a football field in under 10 seconds.

While grizzlies can run 35 mph, black bears are a little slower at 30 mph. There is no racehorse on earth that can beat a bear in a 100-yard dash. The fastest human runners on earth can run 28 mph. The fastest runners on earth will be caught. Running makes it worse.

"Know how to tell the difference between a grizzly and a black bear, greenhorn? Ya climb the nearest aspen tree. If'n it comes up and bites you it's a black bear. If'n it knocks the durn tree over, it's a grizzly."

Grizzly bear

NPS PHOTO BY M. STOUFFER

BIBLIOGRAPHY

Adams, Andy. *The Log of a Cowboy: The Narrative of the Old Trail Days*. Boston: Houghton Mifflin, 2002.

Adams, Ramon F. *A Fitting Death for Billy the Kid*. Norman: University of Oklahoma Press, 1960.

Aikmann, Duncan. *Calamity Jane and the Lady Wildcats*. New York: Henry Holt, 1927.

Armstrong, Erma. "Aunt Ada and the Outlaws: The Story of C. L. Maxwell." *The Outlaw Trail*, Winter 1997.

Arrington, Leonard. *Brigham Young: American Moses*. Urbana: Knopf, 1986.

———. *Great Basin Kingdom: Economic History of the Latter-day Saints, 1830–1900*. Lincoln: University of Nebraska Press, 1958.

Baker, Pearl. *The Wild Bunch at Robbers Roost*. New York: Abelard-Schuman, 1971. Reprint, Lincoln: University of Nebraska Press, 1989.

Betenson, Bill (William). "Lula Parker Betenson." *The Outlaw Trail Journal*, Winter 1995.

Betenson, Lula, and Dora Flack. *Butch Cassidy, My Brother*. Provo, UT: Brigham Young University Press, 1975.

Brier, Warren. "Tilting Skirts and Hurdy-Gurdies: A Commentary on Gold Camp Women." *Montana, The Magazine of Western History*, Autumn 1969.

Brooks, Juanita. *The Mountain Meadows Massacre*. Norman: University of Oklahoma Press, 1962.

Brown, Dee. *The American West*. New York: Charles Scribner's Sons, 1994.

———. *Wondrous Times on the Frontier*. New York: Harper Collins, 1992.

Buck, Daniel, and Anne Meadows. *Digging Up Butch and Sundance*, revised edition. Lincoln, NE: Bison Books, 1996.

———. "Etta Place: A Most Wanted Woman." *Western Outlaw-Lawmen History Association Journal*, vol. 3, no. 1, Spring-Summer 1993.

Burke, John. *Buffalo Bill: The Noblest Whiteskin*. New York: Putnam, 1973.

Burkey, Reverend Blaine. *Wild Bill Hickok: The Law in Hays City*. Hays, KS: T. More Prep., 1973.

Burns, Walter Noble. *The Saga of Billy the Kid*. New York: Grosset and Dunlap, 1926.

Burroughs, John Rolfe. *Where the Old West Stayed Young*. New York: William Morrow and Company, 1962.

Canary, Martha Jane. *Calamity Jane's Letters to Her Daughter*. San Lorenzo, CA: Shameless Hussy Press, 1976.

Chidsey, Donald Barr. *The California Gold Rush*. New York: Crown, 1968.

Davidson, Art. *Sometimes Cassidy*. Salt Lake City: Hawkes Publishing, 1994.

DeJournette, Dick and Jan. *One Hundred Years of Brown's Park and Diamond Mountain*. Vernal, UT: Mansfield Printing, Inc., 1996.

DeVoto, Bernard. *Across the Wide Missouri*. New York: Houghton Mifflin, 1947.

Drago, Gail. *Etta Place: Her Life and Times with Butch Cassidy and the Sundance Kid*. Plano: Republic of Texas Press, 1996.

Dullenty, Jim. *The Butch Cassidy Collection*. Hamilton, MT: Rocky Mountain House Press, 1986.

Dykes, J. C. *Billy the Kid: The Bibliography of a Legend*. Albuquerque: University of New Mexico Press, 1952.

Dykstra, Robert. *The Cattle Towns*. New York: Knopf, 1968.

Faber, Doris. *Calamity Jane: Her Life and Her Legend*. Boston: Houghton Mifflin Company, 1992.

Gray, Dorothy. *Women of the West*. New York: Norton, 1982.

Hawk, Richard Red. *ABC's The American Indian Way*. Sacramento, CA: Sierra Oaks Publishing Co., 1988.

Hertzog, Peter. *Little Known Facts about Billy the Kid*. Santa Fe: Press of the Territorian, 1963.

Kildare, Maurice. "Bear River Loot." *The Real West*, September 1968.

Lamar, Howard R. (ed.). *The Reader's Encyclopedia of the American West*. New Haven, CT: Yale University Press, 1998.

McLaughlin, Marie L. *Myths and Legends of the Sioux*. Lincoln: University of Nebraska Press, 1990.

Meadows, Anne. *Digging Up Butch and Sundance*. New York: St. Martin's Press, 1994.

Morn, Frank. *The Eye That Never Sleeps: A History of the Pinkerton National Detective Agency*. Bloomington: Indiana University Press, 1982.

Pointer, Larry. *In Search of Butch Cassidy*. Norman: University of Oklahoma Press, 1977.

Redford, Robert. *The Outlaw Trail: A Journey Through Time*. New York: Grosset & Dunlap, 1976.

Reiter, Joan Swallow. *The Old West: The Women*. Alexandria: Time Life Books, 1978.

Rosa, Joseph G. *They Called Him Wild Bill: The Life and Adventures of James Butler Hickok*. Norman: University of Oklahoma Press, 1964, 1974.

———. *The Gunfighter: Man or Myth?* Norman: University of Oklahoma Press, 1969.

Rutter, Michael. *Bedside Book of Bad Girls: Outlaw Women of the American West*. Helena, MT: Farcountry Press, 2008.

———. *Boudoirs to Brothels: The Intimate World of Wild West Women*. Helena, MT: Farcountry Press, 2014.

———. *Outlaw Tales of Utah*. Guilford, CT: TwoDot Books, 2011.

———. *Upstairs Girls*. Helena, MT: Farcountry Press, 2004.

———. *Wild Bunch Women*. Guilford, CT: TwoDot Books, 2003.

Sandoz, Mari. *The Battle of Little Bighorn*. Lincoln: University of Nebraska Press, 1978.

Selcer, Richard F. *Hell's Half Acre*. Fort Worth: Texas Christian University Press, 1991.

Stegner, Wallace. *The Gathering of Zion: The Story of the Mormon Trail*. Lincoln: University of Nebraska Press, 1992.

Utley, Robert M. *Billy the Kid: A Short and Violent Life*. Lincoln: University of Nebraska Press, 1989.

———. *Cavalier in Buckskin: George Armstrong Custer and the Western Military Frontier*. Norman: University of Oklahoma Press, 1988.

———. *The Lance and the Shield: The Life and Times of Sitting Bull*. New York: Henry Holt & Co., 1993.

———. *The Last Days of the Sioux Nation*. New Haven, CT: Yale University Press, 1963.

Vestal, Stanley. *Joe Meek: The Merry Mountain Man*. Lincoln: University of Nebraska Press, 1952.

Wilson, John P. *Merchants, Guns & Money: The Story of Lincoln County and Its Wars*. Santa Fe: Museum of New Mexico Press, 1987.

INDEX

ABOUT THE AUTHOR

Michael Rutter is a writer/photographer who has published fifty books and hundreds of articles for magazines, journals, and newspapers.

He is a recipient of the Ben Franklin Book Award for Excellence and the Rocky Mountain Book Publishers' Award. An "addicted" fly fisherman, his outdoor essays have been widely published (from Yale University to *Outdoor Life*). Michael has worked with American Experience on "The Wild West Series" and is interviewed in the A&E documentary *Butch Cassidy and the Sundance Kid* (Netflix, PBS). He has been a Christa McAuliffe Fellow and an AT&T Scholar. He currently consults with Qualtric, specializing in corporate communications and management training.

He spends summers wandering "west" of the Mississippi searching for stories and images—researching, digging into documents, photographing, tracking animals, and throwing copious amounts of fly line. He teaches advanced writing at Brigham Young University, and lives in Orem, Utah, with his wife, Shari, three cats, and a large, very spoiled dog, a Turkish Akbash name Starrfish.

His book titles include: *Boudoirs to Brothels: The Intimate World of Wild West Women*; *Wild Bunch Women* (TwoDot Books); *Upstairs Girls: Prostitution in the American West*; *Outlaw Tales of Utah* (TwoDot Books); *Bedside Book of Bad Girls: Outlaw Women of the American West*; *Fly Fishing Made Easy* (Falcon/ Globe Pequot), and *Utah Off the Beaten Path* (Globe Pequot). He is currently researching nineteenth-century women of Colorado for a new project.